W9-AVY-759

ALSO BY THE AUTHOR

The Hero's Journey: The Life and Work of Joseph Campbell

Riders on the Storm: My Life with Jim Morrison and The Doors (by John Densmore with Phil Cousineau)

DEADLINES

A Rhapsody on a Theme of Famous and Infamous Last Words

BY PHIL COUSINEAU

with woodcuts by Robin Eschner

SISYPHUS PRESS

Sisyphus Press
298 4th Ave., P.O. Box 417
San Francisco, California 94118

LIBRARY OF CONGRESS CATALOGING-IN-PUBLICATION DATA
Cousineau, Phil
Deadlines.
I. Title
1990 90-091643
ISBN 0-9626548-0-9

10 9 8 7 6 5 4 3 2 1

Printed in the United States of America

Design by Eric A. Johnson, Okeanos Press

First published in the United States of America by Sisyphus Press, 1991

Grateful acknowledgement is made to the following for permission to quote from the song: Doors Music Company for "Texas Radio/The Big Beat" copyright © 1968 by Doors Music Co.

Dedicated to my father,
Stanley H. Cousineau,
who taught me the love of words

"Let sons learn from lipless fathers
how man enters hell without a golden bough."

STANLEY KUNITZ

"Throughout the whole of life one must continue
to learn and live and, what will amaze you even more,
one must learn to die."

SENECA

"Death is the mother of beauty."

WALLACE STEVENS

I

Let us praise the torchbearers . . .

ONCE again, the dream:
The plunge, the thieving,
The winged flight from the man with no shadow,
Down to the shadow-strewn room riddled with old crones,
Spinning wheel, poised scissors,
Gold thread, and quicksilver question
That sears my soul,
Seizes my voice:

"*What were you waiting for?*"

Gathered around family deathbeds,
Clinging to life-clenching lovers,
Huddled over dying heroes,
Fingers poised on fading pulses,
Eyes focused on the face of eternity,
Ears hovering over trembling mouths,
Our hearts set sail
As we listen
For the reconciliation,
The necessary words,
The solitary truth,
The supreme dream,
The grief balm,
The last words
That will explain
The lost words
For the first
Time.

The mystery is there
Where the terrible beauty
Of imponderably brief lives
Is condensed into immortal proverbs,

Where epigrams are compressed
From dramatic last moments,
Where last words are saved as if
From a dying species of language,
Where we salvage dying words on our
Lifelong crusade to preserve rare thoughts,

Where we are relic-hunters in search
Of slivers of insight into death,
Archaeologists digging into the grave uncertainties
Within the dark tomb of the human heart,
Road-weary travelers creating brass rubbings
From the carved-stone profiles of monumental ideas,
Surgeons trepanning folklore from the memento mori skull
To release the pressure of death,

All the while vying to make amends
For the pathos of lost words,
The bathos of unlived life.

For the long conversation that resounds
From age to age, the deep memory
Turning on the spiral of the *strong* time,
Breathes new life into old words,
Ferociously reminds the forgetful ones
In each generation of the tortuous path
Of the human race's painstakingly accumulated wisdom,

Recalls how a rabid mob flayed alive Hypatia,
The last librarian of ancient Alexandria,
Before lighting up northern Egypt like a nova
By incinerating the half million brittle papyrus scrolls
Of the most incandescent library
Of the old world.

And how Qin Shi Huangdi, first emperor of China,
Decreed that all books prior to his frenzied reign,
Three thousand years of revered wisdom,
Be burned as he walled in his kingdom,
Annihilated his critics,
Muted the past.

And how the marauding Vikings ransacked
Dark Age Ireland's luminous monasteries,
Burning with a vengeance the scriptorium's
Knots-of-Eternity manuscripts
That vision-silenced monks had spent their lives
Illuminating, unraveling, word by gilded word.

And how Mohammed II, after sacking Constantinople,
Ordered the 120,000 manuscripts of the emperor's library
To be thrown into the sea by his pillaging soldiers.
And how the gold-lusting conquistadors wantonly
Destroyed two thousand years of sacred Mayan texts,
Posing as gods saving pagan souls.

And how during the carnage of Henry VIII's Dissolution,
Medieval Europe's grandest library at Glastonbury Abbey
Was auctioned off for the price of its parchment.

And how the pyromaniacal Inquisition torched
The funeral pyres of condemned alchemists
With the fiery kindling of their own enigmatic notebooks.
And how 19th-century glory-swollen French troops
In their zealous "mission to civilize" in Southeast Asia
Torched the Vietnamese Imperial Library
In unenlightened hopes of cauterizing
The festering wounds
Of colonization.

There is an ancient legend, Kipling recalled,
Of the first adventure and of its returning hero
Who had not the bold words to describe his deeds.
But the squirming silence called for a story.
In his stead there arose a masterless man,
The first storyteller, "afflicted—that is the phrase—
With the magic of the necessary words."
But the tribe so feared the man whose words
"became alive and walked up and down
In the hearts of all his hearers,"
So afraid that he might hand down untrue tales
To their children, that they struck him down.

Only later did they realize that
"The magic was in the words, not the man."

Lost words are cast-off words,
Cast onto the sea of legend
Like jettisoned bottles,
("No food, no water . . .
Wish you were here instead of me!"
Read the last-hope message of the vanished
Traveler Richard Halliburton),
Drifting words destined
For the desert isles of the future
Where Robinson Crusoe readers,
Shipwrecked without a past,
Build fortresses of imagination
From the flotsam of memory and jetsam of ideas
Washed ashore by the tempests of time,
Retrieved by the remembering ones.

For there is a deeper longing than ours alone,
One that moves through us like the doppler effect
Of a long lone train whistle on a sagebrush-blown prairie,
Provokes our wonder about the words that may have purged us
In Sophocles' 116 *lost* plays,
And the rituals that may have initiated us
In the unexcavated memoirs of the last priestess
Of the Eleusinian Mysteries,
And the creation myths that may have inspired us
In the still-silent wooden tablets
And brooding statues of Easter Island,
And the howl of the stalking minotaur
In the lost labyrinth of Crete
That might have inspired the night sea journey in us,
And the erotic ballads of the troubadours
That might have roused the lyrical lover in us,
And the sand paintings that might have healed us,
The courting dances that might have stirred us,

The death songs that might have reconciled us
In the abandoned canyon villages
Of vanished Indian tribes.

And what of all the lost epics by the unknown
Homers and Virgils from the lost civilizations
Still buried in sand, hidden in jungle?

And what was the luring song of the Sirens?
And what of the long years of lost sayings of Christ?
And which question broke the spell of the Waste Land?
And where is St. Brendan's 6th-century log of his voyage to America?
And what was in Lord Byron's memoirs that his heirs had to burn?
And who was the Dark Lady in Shakespeare's sonnets?

And what does "Crotoan" mean,
That confounding last word carved into a tree
By the Roanoke colony that disappeared into oblivion?

And what words did Goethe utter to describe his sudden solitude
As he set down the quill and foolscap and blew the ink dry
After 60 years of wrestling with Mephistopheles in *Faust*?

And what of all the Helen Kellers
Whose hushed songs died with them,
Not having the braille nor the pen to cry: I exist!
Nevertheless her tremulous epiphany in Rodin's lilac-scented
Sculpture garden, when alone with "The Thinker,"
She transmuted her emotions from her probing fingertips
Into the words, the hulking artist later said
Would have taken him 100 years to describe:

"*I feel the throes of the emerging mind . . .* "

Let us praise the torchbearers
(rather than torch the praisesingers)
Who kindled the Promethean gift of fire
In their bellies—where poetry is born—
As well as the fire-fighting monks and scribes,
Scholars, chroniclers, and translators,

Who ferociously struggled to save, rescue, and reclaim
From the winds, flames, and storms of oblivion
The papyrus leaves and vellum scrolls,
The cuneiform tablets and birch-bark fragments,
The calligraphy and petroglyphs, codexes and parchments,
The Upanishads, Gnostic Gospels, and Popol Vuh,

The Rubaiyat, Rosetta Stone, and Book of Kells,
The books wrenched from the prison cells,
Of St. John of the Cross and Cervantes,
And the death camps of Sakharov and Frankl,
The indexes, banned and condemned works
Torn from the icy hands of the censors,
Revisionists, and disinformationists.

What sense can we make out of this preservation
Of words in all their protean forms?
This reading that is like talking to men
Of other centuries, this listening
That is like huddling around the primordial fire
With spellbinding storytellers?
This writing that ignites the coal of imagination
To warm the chilled spaces between us?
This dancing in the soul to the be-bop rhythm
Of the contagious foot-tapping music of the spheres?
This vision questing like the shaman and his taut goatskin drum
Echoing the heartbeat of the world?

Do we not save certain charmed words and talismanic stories
As if they were ancient sites, threatened monuments
That have outlasted empires and emperors,
Crumbling moonlit temples of ancestral thought,
Which we protect and restore and pilgrimage to,
(like the delirious Piranesi with his coal-dark sketchbooks
"Prowling for the ineffable" through Rome's tumbledown glories),
Because they are *survivors*, evidence of the past, foundations
For the future, symbols for conquering time and space?

And like those imagination-roiling ruins
At Glastonbury, Jericho, Karnak, and Stonehenge,
That outlasted the grave robbers and death warrants,
Ruins that now haunt us, taunt us, to be deciphered,
Tantalizing stones silhouetted against mortality itself,

Last words stand for lost thoughts,
Wandering sounds reverberating
Long after iconic lives
Fade far away.

From the nave to the grave
We vibrate like tuning forks
To the euphonious sounds and elegant shapes,
The mellifluous taste and reeling smells,
The very spin and color of white-heat words
Shimmering across the Sahara of silence,

Proving that the world is indeed
made up of stories
and not atoms.

"Tis you then burned the library?"
bellowed the horrified Victor Hugo,
"You have quenched the light in your own soul!"

"I did, I brought the fire,"
the arsonist replied torpidly.
"*I can't read*."

Revel we do
Before ecstatic language
That pries open a crack into the past,
Bends time to suggest the future,
Reminds us like a clarion bell from a distant valley,
That although Bolivian Indians may have 200 words for potatoes,
And the Eskimos 93 words for snow,
And the Hindus 108 words for the Ganges,
And the English 228 words for drinking,
And the Germans 30 words for kissing,
And the Arabs 204 words for camels,
And the Sufis 99 names for God,
There are countless synonyms for last words,

The longed-for summing-up of our lives,
Exquisite but exasperating hints of the final stirring
That the sages speak of by many names,
As with Matthew Arnold who said,

"*Truth sits upon the lips of dying men.*"

So we can take to heart the final phrases of others
As *l'esprit d'escalier*, the wit of the staircase,
(The smooth repartee of things we wish we had said
But remember too late—as we are leaving),
An echo of the universal belief in the power of the word
To ward off—or familiarize us with—the unknown,

Like Scheherazade mesmerizing the Sultan
By spinning life-saving stories
For a thousand and one sultry nights.
Or Aesop, the liberated slave,
Who collected, as the ancients would have it,
His wild-tongued fables from the peasants
In the fields and the animals in the woods,
Then bartered the tales for food and drink and shelter
As he wandered the sun-baked roads of classical Greece.

Or the Hindu medicine men who prescribed
A holy story along with their herbs
To heal body and soul together.
Or the warriors of ancient Syracuse who offered to release
Their Greek prisoners during the Peloponnesian Wars
If they could recite 10 memorable lines from a Greek play.

Or the Comanche raiders who stuffed their bullhide shields
With paper from scavenged books along their raiding trail
Because the compressed pages were nearly bullet-proof,
Startling at least one rancher who captured a shield
That was padded with layers of rawhide, feathers, hair—
And a complete history of Rome.

Or the French philosopher Pascal who sewed a note
Into his coat lining that was found after his death: the amulet
Of the hidden revelation, the vision of fire, "the tears of joy,"

That broke the fever of his long illness and inspired
His masterpiece reflections, the *Pensées*.

Or the German playwright Ernest Toller who was sentenced
By the Nazis to eat his own words—page by page—
As punishment for his anti-Fascist speeches.
Or the incarcerated Russian poet Irina Ratushinskaya,
Who secretly etched her poetry into bars of soap
With the flaring ends of matchsticks,
Quickly learned her words by heart
Then washed them away to avoid
Confiscation by the guards.

Or the Kenyan playwright Ngũgũ Wa Thiong'o,
Who scribbled his *Free Thoughts on Toilet Paper*
While imprisoned for sedition.

Or the Irish wordwizard James Joyce
Who admitted to capriciously working
Enough enigmas and riddles into *Ulysses*
To bewilder scholars for centuries,
Their gnomic debates thus
Sealing his immortality.

Or Michael Rennie in *The Day the Earth Stood Still*,
Invoking the incantatory "*Klatu barada niktu*"
To stave off catastrophe for earthlings slouching toward apocalypse.

Or the legendary printer who brooded over the loss
Of the woman he loved until he set her name in lead type
And swallowed it so he would never lose her again.

Or the Mexican lovers on the Day of the Dead festival
Who carve their names in icing on tiny skulls of sugar,
Then slowly eat them to sweeten their death-defying passion.

Or the Druid initiates who were bound
By their spiral-wanded, dragon-master priests
To cliffside rockingstones on rain-lashed nights
Believing they would awake
    Either dead,
    Mad, or a poet.

✤

In the beginning was the Word
And in the end will be the word,
Written down—and perhaps embellished—
By our survivors who will wrest it
From the belljar silence of our sudden absence
Because for every word ever uttered
There is an anti-word,
The word unsaid,
Inaudible,
Unexpressed,
Inarticulated.

And as we wait in between heartbeats,
(The moment Japanese calligraphers put swirling ink to paper),
The gulag prisoner in solitary confinement
Who saved 30,000 Jews in World War II
Taps gingerly on the metal pipes
A message no one will ever decode—

And yet the black chord hovers,
The pulverizing truth,
The triumphant requiem
For the funeral
Of the resistance movement
Of all those who struggle
To revive the fading words,
To resurrect the disintegrating words,
To reinvent the words
That never lived at all,
To honor the words that died on the tongue,
To anticipate which words will live beyond the grave.

And still he waits
To hear us strike the white chord,
The soaring notes

To forgive the words that betrayed us,
To forgive ourselves for the words we used to betray,
To remind ourselves that there
Is less time than we think

To explain ourselves to each other,
To put death off the scent
While we flesh out our hollow selves,
To say what we must
To authenticate our lives.

To answer Claude Simon, the trench-weary survivor of the carnage
Of the Flanders road, who challenged his father's sorrow
Over the cindered books of Leipzig's bombed-out library,
Because he numbly felt the precious knowledge within its walls
Had been powerless against the chicanery of evil
During the berserk "war to end all wars."

To run inside the slipstream of history
That Orwell prophetically wrote was
"A race between education and catastrophe."

To learn the old ways
Of the Apache prisoner who vowed,
"I will keep my word until the stones melt."

There is a collision
In the dark night
And we are it

There is a grappling
Just before dawn
And we are there

There is an urge to put our head
Into the lion's mouth
And it should not be tamed

There is a fury
In the soul
But that is our chance

We must learn
Like the survivors in the gulag
To die one minute and dance the next

"Why, Death,
Must you be the one
To teach me life?"

Night after black-winged night
I am in the dream café
hearing my owl-voiced father
from his workbench in the winter-chilled basement
hooting at me through the heating vents,

*"Any famous last words, Philip,
before you go to sleep?"*

If the pen is indeed
The tongue of the mind,
Then words are the fingers,
Reaching, groping, touching
Metaphors for who we are,
Messengers across the numinous abyss
To other people, times, places,
And our interminable wrestling with them
Is the lifelong resistance
Of sphinx-like silence
To surrender the mystery
Before the blue vein
Runs dry,
Before the violet energy
Runs down,
Before the russet dream
Runs away.

"And when I have fears that I will cease to be
Before my pen has glean'd
My teeming brain . . . "

I will fill the thirsty inkwell
With black blood squeezed

From dark stone
And write myself back to life
From the still point in the dance
Until the stunning warning
Is heard no more—

"*You have not plunged deep enough.*"

On a night vertiginous with shimmering constellations,
The Perseid meteors streaking across the dark dome of sky,
The Andromeda galaxy pinwheeling overhead
Two million light-years away,
You turn to me before the sweet-smelling turf fire,
Wipe the lovesweat from off your brow,
Place my hand on your still-racing heart,
So I might remember
How wordless we were
When we like Sisyphus
Stunned Hades and froze time,
Stalled for a precipitous moment
Our spiraling fall,
Time's inevitable lunge:

How we then gasped
With the dark thirst,
Heard in the bloodsurge
What we could not describe,
The seething teeming silence
Behind words,
Beyond self.

The soul is a green piano
That plays in the key of blue
Beyond the long red deadline

II

"The soul may be the part of you that sees the dream"

LISTEN: a story is working its way up and out like shrapnel:
Long ago Eros took refuge from the blistering sun
In the cool cave of Hades himself,
And in his collapse to the cave floor unwittingly scattered
His arrows among those of the god of the underworld:
And that is why love and death are found in the same quiver.

The heart of the mind is not matter,
The mind of the matter is not heart,
The heart of the matter is imagination,
There beyond the maps of reason
In the undiscovered
Image:

Where the old archaeologist's sunburned hand
Is tentatively probing the hot desert sand when suddenly
He is cut by the sharp edge of the long-buried tablet,
His blood seeping down into the 3500-year-old Sumerian runes
As he translates the timeworn words, feels the shock
Of recognition of his own dilemma, panics when he realizes
There is a missing shard to the tablet containing the answer
Of the old sage to Gilgamesh's anguished question:

"*How do I find the life for which I am searching?*"

In the penumbra of last words
Is a fear of death,
The terror of life,
The unburdened heart,
The unrevealed mystery,
The unvanquished foes,
The unmet friends,
The unmanifested dreams,
The unsired children,

The unseen beauty,
The unsung love,
The unspoken word.

In the aurora of last words
Is the allure of death,
The awe of life,
The shadowboxing with eternity,
The bullfighting with infinity,
The remasking of the gods,
The revisioning of forms,
The recreated mysteries,
The revealed passions,
The rebirth of language.

And so we muse over the words of Montaigne,
"He who would teach men how to die
Would teach them how to live."

And ruminate over the last letter
Of Sir Walter Raleigh while he waited
For the razor's kiss of the widow-maker
In the Tower of London,
"It is death alone
That can make a man
Suddenly know himself."

And mull over the request
Of the earnestly questing reporter
In the smoke-shrouded pressroom of *Citizen Kane*,
"What were the last words Kane said on earth?
Maybe he told us all about himself
On his deathbed?"

According to Herodotus, the Greek historian,
The first word uttered by the human race
Was *becos*, the Phrygian word for "bread."

Who will be listening for the last word?

After the anthropologist had descended from the clouds
In his roaring bird-beast-helicopter and trekked through
The green heart of the rain forest to the cliffside cave
Of the Stone Age Tasaday tribe, he hesitantly asked
Their deep-browed chief storyteller to describe the soul,
And the old seer pondered, then replied,

"*The soul may be the part of you that sees the dream.*"

In those heart-quickening
Moments of absolute certainty
When a fine line, a keen word,
An urgent story,
Finds an echo in you,
Have you asked yourself
Who is dreaming who—
If you are dreaming the world
Or the world is dreaming you?

Have you not heard
The bison-rumble of time
While marooned in fogbound bog?
Have you not thrown
Thought-curves
At the Lords of Death?

Have you not tasted
The salty tongue
Of the late-night visitor?

Have you not turned the skeleton key?

It is nearly dawn in Liberty, Texas,
A backwater town of clapboard shacks, tire-swings

And dark green praying mantis-like oil derricks.
I fill up the car from a gurgling six-foot glass pump
While a crackling radio plays "Crazy" by Patsy Cline,
And the grease-barnacled owner named Morry
Takes over-the-shoulder slugs of Jack Daniels.
He mumbles the lyrics while blinking back face-rusting tears,
Waits for the bluesy lost-lover anthem to shiver to a close,
Then suddenly confesses to me in a gravelly, stutter-stepping voice,
"If I knew I was going to kick the bucket tomorrow I reckon
I'd change everything: my job, my old lady, my life."
The cigarette butt flares as it burns down to his fingers.
His eyes glaze over like a hunting dog frozen in point,
A neighbor whose house is burning down now.

At dusk in the tangled rush-hour traffic of Manhattan,
A cab driver harrumphs to a *Life* magazine reporter
Who is interviewing him about the meaning of life,
"We're here to die, just to live and die.
I do some fishing, take my girl out, pay taxes,
Then get ready to drop dead."

In Stockholm a century earlier, chemist and inventor
Alfred Nobel one morning at breakfast was startled
To read his own obituary, and discovered to his horror
That he had been eulogized not for his creations,
His philanthropy or compassion, but for the destruction
He had wrought in his life, only for his invention
Of dynamite, only as a merchant of death.

What will it take for us to *see* with the piercing eyes
Of the weaver behind the red-threaded loom
In the royal tapestry factory?
To gaze in the sacred manner
Of the Indian medicine men over
The holy land of the ancestors?
To trust the animal eye, focus the primal vision?
To give birth to the god within
Through our immaculate perception?

To find the woodcutter's path in the dark forest?
To live as if our life depended on it?
To feel beneath the torpor?
To break the deadbolt?
To realize that death is more universal than life
Only because not everybody *lives*?

To stand with Rilke before
The luminous statue of Apollo,
The elegiac ruins at Duino,
The pulsating oranges of Cézanne,
The swaggering panther of the Paris zoo,
Until we see with heart-thrumming clarity that

"*You must change your life.*"

Last words are the last act of the mystery play,
Lines that can be read as the universal drama
Of self-revelation, a diorama of a human being's final moments
Replete with the *megaphors*, the monumental phrases,
The verbal *trompe l'oeils*, the brilliant word illusions,
The three-dimensional renderings of the *hermetic* questions,
(The ones we were dying to ask),
The crack-in-the-floorboard answers
(The ones we were dying to hear),
The sudden character motivations
That illuminate our own conflicts
And stun us with the blood memory,
The fevered flow of the blood line,

Underscore the philosopher who confessed that most people—
Including himself—spend much of their lives
Talking around what they really want to say:

A vivid illustration of how a few intimate words
May convey as much as a lifetime of headlines,
A few italicized words mean more than a career of fine print.

These dramatic third act realizations
Push us to the edge of our seat

With the white-knuckled hope for catharsis
From memorable story lines that might
Wrestle immortality from anonymity,
Fight against the common grave,
Provoke us into rethinking our lives
With their whiplashing last lines, punchlines,
And deadlines:

Like the man of silence, exile and cunning, James Joyce,
Who forged a new consciousness in literature
In the smithy of his melancholic Celtic soul,
Then died in a firestorm of doubt,
Asking even his devoted wife Nora,
"Does nobody understand?"

And the dialectical philosopher George Hegel,
Whose final synthesis was finally understandable,
"Only one man ever understood me . . .
And he didn't understand me."
And the redoubtable Dutch scholar Hugo Grotius,
"By understanding many things
I have accomplished nothing."
And the condemned Irish patriot Roger Casement in a last letter,
"It is a cruel thing to die with all men misunderstanding."
And the poet-dramatist Heinrich Schiller
Who sought to distill beauty from his own death,
"Many things are growing plain and clear to my understanding."

And the wanderlusting Marco Polo,
Who regretted in his last hours,
"I did not write half of what I saw."
And the star-struck astronomer Pierre Simon LaPlace,
"What we know is not much;
What we do not know is immense."
And the relative-minded Albert Einstein,
"And even so I've not quite convinced myself
That it is all true."
And the inscrutable Leonardo da Vinci,
"I have offended God and man because my work
Wasn't good enough . . . tell me ever . . .
If things were done."
And the saturnine Michelangelo,
"Weary, weary . . . My soul I resign to God,

My body to the earth, my worldly goods to my next of kin."
And the imponderable Plotinus,
"I am making my last effort to return that which is divine in me
To that which is divine in the universe."
And the mystical Thomas Merton,
"Soon I will disappear from view . . . "

And the mathematician Evariste Galois,
Having fatally miscalculated in a duel to the death,
"Don't cry. I need all my courage to die at twenty."
And the Greek philosopher Phocion
After a kangaroo court sentencing,
"All the great men of Athens have met the same end."
And the rapier-witted French writer Roch Chamfort,
Preferring suicide to execution by the tribunal,
"Ah, my friend, I am about to leave this world
Where the heart must either be broken or of brass."
And the eagle-proud Geronimo
To his stone-souled U.S. Army captors,
"I want to go back to my old home before I die."

And the gold-nosed medieval astronomer Tycho Brahe,
Turning his telescope back on his own life,
"Let me not seem to have died in vain."
And the peripatetic warrior-poet T. E. Lawrence (of Arabia),
"There is something broken in the works,
The will, I think."
And the cavalry-haunted Chief Joseph of the Nez Percé,
Begging his son not to sign any more treaties with white men,
". . . never sell the bones of your father and mother."

Or the missionary-cursed Hawaiian King Kalakaua,
"I tried to restore our gods, our way of life . . . "
Or the vision-gouged Vincent van Gogh,
"I shall never be rid of this depression."
Or the raven-haunted Edgar Allen Poe,
"Lord, help my poor soul."

Or the lugubrious Alfred Hitchcock,
"I am a sea of alone."
Or the glorious John Keats,
"Don't breathe on me—it comes like ice."
Or the humorless Demonax,

"Draw the curtains—the farce is over."
Or the contumelious Auguste Comte,
"What an irreparable loss."
Or the pious Joseph Addison,
"See in what peace a Christian can die."
Or the portentous George Jackson,
"The dragon has come."
Or the gangrenous Rabelais,
"I go to seek the great perhaps."
Or the adventurous Thomas Hobbes,
"I am about to take my last voyage,
A great leap in the dark."

Or the puckish Alan Watts,
Remarking with irreducible rascality,
"Life is like a bubble—*poof*—
And it's gone."
Or the mischievous André Gide,
Powdered and rehearsed for immortality,
"I'm afraid my sentences
Are becoming grammatically incorrect . . .
Before you quote me make sure I'm conscious."

Or the audacious Galileo,
"*Eppur si muove*,"
"Still it moves."

Between dream and waking
Life and death
Companionship and solitude
Is the *third thing*
The imagining
That last words point
Toward first:

For what's a metaphor
But to touch the black cat
In the dark room that isn't there?
To assemble the ship of death

In the bottle of life
That has no sides?

To reconcile ourselves
With the stones?
To bend our minds
To keep knowledge from blinding us?
To squeeze the precise words in
In time in the space allotted to us
As the deadline approaches
As fast as groundrush
To a tumbling
Paratrooper?

Long after the unexpected death,
In the long-unopened book with the sepia cover photo
Of Ankor Wat, the enchanted Cambodian temple rediscovered
Beneath the nightmare of history's stone-strangling vines,
He found the unread letter from his father,
Unsteady words in dark red ink that asked,

"*Did my love of words influence you?*"
And emotion burst like a blood vessel:
He had the vain illusion he had been all alone.

The son who wears his father's soul
Passes on the gathered wisdom and can sit
In the circle of drummers with the village elders.

The brute truth
Lingers there where
The dream prowls

There where wonder
Swirls in
The wound

There in the dark time
When the eye begins to hear

And the ear begins to see
Where the lungs feel
And the heart breathes
There while soul is shaped

The hobbled
Conquistador waits alone
By the still windmills

Listen:
The mesmerizing cry from the minaret
Propping up the ruins of the heart:
"No one knows our name
Until the last
Breath."

III

Plato, with the satires of Sophron under his pillow as he lay dying, condensed his life's work into two words: "Practice Dying."

PLATO, with the satires of Sophron under his pillow
As he lay dying, condensed his life's work
Into two words: "Practice Dying."
Socrates, hoping to allay his friends' fears
When they revealed to him that the 30 grim judges of Athens
Had condemned him to death, calmly replied, "And nature them."
Ancient Egyptians ritualistically propped up a skeleton
In the chair of honor at banquet tables to remind revelers
Of their own mortality, that, All is vanity.
The Scandinavians of old imagined Odin the All-Wise,
God of wisdom, poetry, war, and agriculture,
As sitting underneath the gallows for inspiration from the dead.

Montaigne, while other intrepid Europeans were exploring
Spice routes and silk roads, retreated to his
Book-lined belvedere in his secluded Dordogne château
To essay into the "terra incognita of his own mind,"
And summed up his mental peregrinations by writing,
"To philosophize is to learn how to die."
Balzac, on a visit to Napoleon's necropolis, Père Lachaise cemetery,
Confided to a companion, among the crypts and chestnut trees,
"While seeking out the dead, I see nothing but the living."
And Sarah Bernhardt once declared to mortified friends that she
Slept in a satin-lined coffin the night before a performance,
"So I can put more life into the drama."

Down the long flume
Of history, it appears
The world speaks in allegories
Of how a descent into hell
Endows us with an odd
Power of speech,

And how the craft of life
Demands from us
The art of dying.

✜

Ever since death first stirred astonishment,
Evoked grief, moved the human heart to strew
Roses, amaranths, myrtle and marigolds into a grave
To accompany the dead into the underworld of the shades,
Or honor Hermes, the guide of souls into the arms of Hades,
By placing fertility stones at the vital crossroads,
The ineffable disappearing act of human beings
Has been the prime mover of religion, mythology and art,
A brazen eraser that wipes away the past,
But holds within its black folds
The traces of a life's experience,
The white dust from which the world arises anew.

The primal terror—and utter fascination—with death
Is a conflagration in the fiery bowels of life,
The very center of the cyclone
Where creation and destruction collide,
And the world ear is pitched for the key of mystery,
And the timeless eye that *looks back* at us
From the words with the gargoyle-gaze,
That test our capacity for compassion,
Those words that trick the mind
Into examining the chaos
In other men's hearts,
So we might know our own:

As with the paragon of paranoia, Franz Kafka,
Who pleaded with a friend to strike all his manuscripts
From the records of his lifelong trial with literature so
"There will be no proof I ever was a writer,"
Then was so repulsed by the stench of his final verdict,
He hurled his ice pack at his doctor while screaming,
"No more torture . . . Why prolong it? . . . But don't go away. . . . "

Or the lecherous but contrite Marquis de Sade,
Who requested in his last will and testament that
"The ground over my grave shall be sprinkled with acorns
So that all traces of it shall disappear and I hope,
Any reminder of my existence may be wiped out
From the memory of mankind."

Or the flapper novelist Djuna Barnes protesting
On her deathbed that old people should be killed,
"There should be a law! This business of helping them
Stay alive—it's inhuman! I'm already lost!
Do you know that? I've already died
And they brought me back. It's terrible."

Or the florid English artist Aubrey Beardsley,
"I am imploring you—burn all the indecent poems and drawings!"
Or the lawyer William Lloyd Garrison,
When asked by his doctor if there was anything to be done,
"Finish it up!"
Or the Victorian artist-craftsman William Morris,
"I want the mumbo-jumbo out of this world!"
Or the self-cultivated curmudgeon writer Wyndham Lewis,
Who barked to his nurse when she asked about his bowels,
"Mind your own business!"
Or the Gothic scene-chewer Joan Crawford,
Shrieking to her daughter,
"Don't you dare ask God to help me!"
Or Clara Barton, unable to nurse herself back to health,
"Let me go! Let me go!"
Or the Italian playwright Gabriele D'Annunzio,
Barking at his chauffeur,
"Stop! Turn home! . . . I'm bored . . . I'm bored. . . . "

Or Abdur Rahman Khan, emir of 19th-century Afghanistan,
"My last words to my son and successor are:
'Never trust the Russians!' "
Or the profligate Roman emperor Severus,
"I have been all things—and it has profited nothing!
Little urn, you will soon hold all that will remain
Of him whom the world could not contain."
Or Princesse de Lamballe, when ordered by the mob
To salute the revolutionary nation,
"Fie on the horror!"
Or the abolitionist John Brown, to his hangman,
"Make it quick!"

Or the irreconcilable Stonewall Jackson,
"I have only two regrets:
That I have not shot Henry Clay or hanged John C. Calhoun."
Or the Wild West bandit Jack "Three-Fingered" Garcia,

"I will throw my hands up for no gringo dog!"
Or the remorseless mass murderer Carl Panzram,
"Hurry it up, you Hoosier bastards.
I could hang a dozen men while you're fooling around!"
Or the French anarchist Jean Messeliers,
"I should like to see the last King
Strangled with the guts of the last priest."
Or the ruthless Ramón María Navarre,
"I do not have to forgive my enemies.
I killed them all."
Or the bellicose explorer Ferdinand de Beagle,
Square-shouldered and cursing before a Chad firing squad,
"I must die . . . *c'est bien* . . . but a Frenchman
Does not fear death . . . I will be revenged."
Or the overly sensitive pickpocket, Thomas B. Moran,
"I've never forgiven that smart-alecky reporter
Who named me 'Butterfingers'—to me it's not funny."

Or the gunned-down convict Bernard Coy,
Captured outside the walls of Alcatraz,
"It don't matter. I figure
I licked the Rock anyway."
Or the journalist H. L. Mencken to his friend James T. Farrell,
"Remember me to my friends; tell them I'm a helluva mess."
Or producer Harry ("I don't get ulcers, I give them") Cohn,
"It's just too tough . . . it's no use . . . get the box. . . . "
Or Harry Houdini, woozy from a failed stunt in Detroit,
And chained to a hospital bed from which there was no escape,
"I'm tired of fighting. I guess this thing is going to get me."

Or the irascible playwright George Bernard Shaw,
Who forgot one of his own best lines, "All is well that ends"
While chastising his nurse at his own final curtain call,
"Sister, you're trying to keep me alive
As an old curiosity, but I'm done,
I'm finished, I'm going to die."

Or the 8th-century Arab military leader
Abd al-rahman, who mourned in his final hours,
"I have now reigned above fifty years in victory or peace.
And I have diligently numbered the days of pure and genuine
Happiness which have fallen to my lot: they amount to
Fourteen—O, man! place not thy confidence in this world."

✣

So even though Mark Twain warned about the dubious nature
Of deathbed conversions and infamous last words when he wrote,
"Many a notorious coward, many a chicken-hearted poltroon,
Coarse, brutal, degraded, has made a dying speech
Without a quaver in his voice and been swung into eternity
With what looked like the calmest fortitude,"

We are voyeurs of the afterlife,
Our eye to the hole-in-the-wall,
Hoping that flirtatious death will disrobe for us
And reveal hot-blooded life;
Rubberneckers of calamity
Incorrigibly peering over our shoulders
To see the frosted words on the telegram
Left by the shrieking traveler in the train station;
Egregiously irreverent scrutinizers
Of the carnage in the streets,
The gore on the screen,
The travesties in the tabloids;

All these ruses
To see what is not spoken about,
As if needing to cheat for a final exam,
Because we're secretly dying to overhear
How others succumbed to the Grim Reaper's
Benignly indifferent harvest,

Whether dryly like the host of the doomed dinner party
In Monty Python's *The Meaning of Life*, saying of Mr. Death,
"He casts a gloom on things, doesn't he?"
Or ironically like Eugene O'Neill,
"Born in a hotel room—and damn it—
Died in a hotel room."
Or pettily like the Spanish writer Lope de Vega,
Credited with 1600 plays in the 16th century,
"All right, then, I'll say it. Dante makes me sick."

Or contentiously like Norwegian playwright Henrik Ibsen,
"On the contrary."
Or dismissively like Swedish playwright Auguste Strindberg,

"Don't worry about me. I'm no longer here."
Or ontologically like Bernard de Fontanelle,
"I feel nothing except a certain difficulty in continuing to exist."
Or cynically like Crato of ancient Thebes,
"You are going, noble hunchback, you are going
To Pluto's Realm, bent double by age."

Or solipsistically like Jonathan Swift,
"I'm a fool . . . I am what I am . . . what I am. . . ."
Or theosophically like Madame Blavatsky,
"I do my best, doctor."
Or ambiguously like humorist James Thurber,
"God bless . . . God damn. . . ."
Or apologetically like Supreme Court Justice John Marshall,
"Goodbye, I'm sorry to have kept you all waiting. So long."
Or blithely like the original Zippy the Pinhead
To his boss of 67 years, P. T. Barnum,
"Well, we fooled 'em for a long time."
Or greedily like Barnum himself,
"Did you count the receipts tonight?"
Or derivatively like the matador José González
"Look at me, I'm dying like Manolete!"
Or avidly like the bankrupt André Citroën,
"After I'm gone the House of Citroën will fall!"
Or revolutionarily like Mexican rebel Emiliano Zapata,
"Better a fighting death than a slave's life."
Or imperiously like Henry VIII,
"All is lost! Monks! Monks! Monks!"

Or jadedly like French general Pierre Cambronne,
"Ah, mademoiselle, man is thought to be something, but he is nothing."
Or alarmingly like Senator Thomas Benton,
"Did you hear that, Kitty? That is the death rattle!"
Or hallucinogenically like the mad dancer Diaghilev,
"They were white . . . all white . . .
They were so white."

Or superstitiously like mystery writer Dashiell Hammett,
Who believed in words in books but suspected them in life,
According to Lillian Hellman who asked him if he needed
To say anything about his dying,
"No, my only chance is
Not to talk about it."

Or hopefully like the Italian sculptor Giacometti,
"Till tomorrow . . . "
Or mulishly like the first Christian Scientist,
Mary Baker Eddy, who refused medical help or solace
By clamming up on her deathbed,
"—."

Running across last words
Is like the sudden *bump* in the night
From driving over an unseen animal
On a dark country road:
A shiver quivering through the tire
Up through the floorboards
To the brake pedal,
Then whipping through your foot,
Climbing up your leg
To grip your heaving heart
With a fist of clenched meaning
From the unknown source—

For these lines call to us
To beware of the one-eyed life,
The unused second sight,

To recall how Spider Grandmother exiled the first Hopis by saying,
"You have forgotten what you should have remembered,
And now you have to leave this place. Things will be harder."

To listen to the coaxing of the jaguar-souled *sensei*
Sparring with you in the training room with poised sword,
"Now all that is left is for you to become yourself."

To read between the lines of the old Pony Express ad:
"WANTED: Young, skinny, wiry fellows not over eighteen.
Must be expert riders willing to risk death daily."

Roped to the masthead
Through the maelstrom
Of the Siren's tantalizing song
Like Odysseus on his fast black ship
As Turner on the canvas
Or Muir on Half Dome
To understand the verticality
The density, the folding over
Discovered in the hemorrhaging sunset
To touch the white noise of our lies
Taste life in the salt
Of the dead sea

"In this world there is no greater pleasure,"
the old translator read with the shock of recognition,
"than coming back to life after being torn to pieces."

On the other side of silence
in a sacred grove of oak trees
humming megaliths and poised horses
waits the muse
who dreams you
to life

What do you say to her
when you finally see her
that won't turn you into a stag?

Here is where you enter the cave or turn back
take the draught of long oblivion
seize a branch of the golden bough

Now you will need all your courage
to let yourself drop
into wine-dark dream

✣

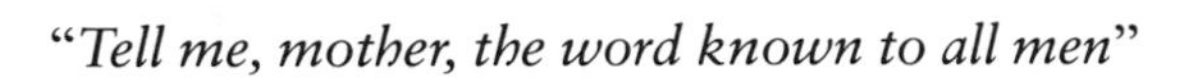

"Tell me, mother, the word known to all men"

Beyond despair
Is subversion—
Astound me

IV

Above the patchquilt green plains of County Lough, in a cemetery of lichen-encrusted granite tombstones, the wind howls of essential things.

THIS descent down into the catacombs of language,
This midnight stroll through the sorcerer's den of words,
This necromancer's apprenticeship on death mask phrases,
This geomancer's angling of tombstones to find the dragon lines,
These lucubrations on the Pantheon of quotes,
These sepulchral thoughts and exit-lines stage left,
These finish-line calls that break the dead-heat,
These spelunking expeditions down into cave pool imagery,
These Outback explorations along the Ancestor's songlines.

These word-divinings to find the life-giving springs,
These death sentences to be pardoned,
Are attempts to raise the Lazarus in myself.

During the Middle Ages the Bretons were compelled
To make the *Tra Breiz*, the pilgrimage round
Of visits to the cathedrals of Brittany
To pay homage to their ancestors.
Whosoever failed to do so in this life,
It was ardently believed, was destined
To complete the journey in the next,
When the sojourn would then only progress
The length of the pilgrim's coffin every seven years.

Above the patchquilt green plains of County Lough,
In a cemetery of lichen-encrusted granite tombstones,
The wind howls of essential things.
Scattered about me are fern-licked slabs of slate,
Finely sculpted Celtic crosses, crumbled boulder gravestones,
Pine-lined crypts, limestone-and-moss family plots.
"In the olden days," the caretaker intones in a proud brogue,
"when a man died, his family would mark his grave
With a stone from his field. And every time they
Would visit it they would tell a story about him.

Mark my words, lad, how else would we remember him?
Now could ye tell me that?"

From his crepe-papered, opium-pungent room
On the Ile St. Louis in 19th-century Paris,
The young spirit-ravaged Charles Baudelaire wrote,
"Death is an angel whose magnetic palms
Bring dreams of ecstasy and slumberous calms
To smooth the hell of poor and naked men."
The word-drunk poet later died in agonizing speechlessness,
Arguing with the photographer Nadar over the existence
Of God by simply pointing towards the rising sun.

"Wake up!" screams Jim Morrison, the black leather lizard king poet,
And the back of your neck burns like a branding.
"No eternal reward will forgive us for wasting the dawn!"

And the Gospels admonish us that "Man is asleep."
". . . a waking sleep," warn the Russian mystics.
And Macbeth hears, "Sleep no more."

And the curious lullaby becomes curiouser
And curiouser and softens your resistance,
"May I wake before I die. . . . "

And the metronomic tick-tock, tick-tock,
Tick-tock of the rosewood grandfather clock
Vibrates in the bones of your ears
And down the curved hallway,
Then pauses to taste its hands,
And you hear it ask,
"What have you done lately to stop me,
To stop my razor-edged hands
Of time?"

The deadwood words burn on,
The phosphorous glow of the fabulator's tales
Reflecting our reptilian brain's
Fear of dying in our sleep, of being buried alive,
Of squandering our time, of time being cut off on us,

Of having had only one turn of the kaleidoscope,
Of being Rip-Van-Winkled out of precious years.
And then it is time,
For time,

The silent language, to end,
As it does every moment,
But some moments more convoluted than others,

As it was for the condemned but uncondemning Socrates
Who thought of an offering to the god of healing
While the hemlock was being carried into his chambers,
"Crito, we ought to give a cock to Asclepius."
Or Sir Thomas More who beseeched his executioner,
"I pray you let me lay my beard over the block
Lest ye should cut it off."
Or Marie Antoinette who stepped on the foot
Of her executioner, Monsieur Paris,
"I beg your pardon. I did not mean it."
Or the leader of the Revolution, Danton,
"Display my head to the crowd—it is worth it.
It will be some time before they see its like again."
Or Charlotte Corday, Marat's assassin,
Transfixed by the gleaming blade of the guillotine,
"I have a right to be curious. I have never seen one before.
It is the toilette of death. But it leads to immortality."
Or the French traitor Le Bodoyere who touched his heart
While lecturing the firing squad,
"This is what you must not miss."
Or the Czechoslovakian patriot John Ziska,
"Make my skin into drumheads for the Bohemian cause!"
Or the chivalrous Sir Walter Raleigh,
"It matters little how the head lies, so the heart be right."
Or the delicate Anne Boleyn who purred,
"My neck is slender."

Or the broiled-alive Christian martyr Saint Lawrence,
"This side is roasted enough. Turn me up, O' tyrant great,
Assay whether roasted or raw thou thinkest the best meat."
Or the pious Saint Boniface as hot lead poured down his throat,
"I thank thee, Lord Jesus, Son of the living God."
Or the outraged Saint Agatha as she was disfigured,
"Cruel tyrant, do you not blush to torture this part of my body?

You who sucked the breasts of a woman yourself?"
Or Joan of Arc, her eyes lifted to heaven
As flames licked at her feet,
"Ah, Rouen, I have great fear that you will suffer
By my death . . . Jesus, Jesus . . . ."

Or Mata Hari, costumed in white gloves and furs,
Her raging beauty and icy calm before the death squad
Causing the captain's sword to rattle in his scabbard
And eight of the twelve riflemen to miss her,
"*Merci, monsieur.*
Vive l'Allemagne!"

The conquering of time and space,
Aye, there's the rub,
The turning over of the hourglass,
The seizing of the day,
The *synesthesia* of overlapping senses,
The undercurrents of magnetic wisdom,
The immortality of memory curled back in on itself,
The remembering, the being remembered,
The caprice of swimming against the dark wave,

The bright lantern of Diogenes,
"One brother anticipates the other: Sleep before Death.
Everything will shortly be turned upside down."
The nostalgia of John Walcott,
When asked if he needed anything,
"Bring back my youth."
The reluctance of Queen Elizabeth I,
Who pleaded with her minions,
"All my possessions for a moment of time."
The scholarly review of Cecil Rhodes
(Or Alexander Graham Bell),
"So little done, so much to do."
The tempo of composer Alban Berg,
"But I have so little time."
The injustice felt by poet Guillaume Apollinaire,
"Save me, doctor. I want to live!
I still have so many things to say!"

The eschatology of Henry David Thoreau,
Who said when asked about the afterlife,
"One world at a time."

The reprieve of Mark Twain
Who confided to a reporter late in life,
"Reports of my death have been greatly exaggerated."

The plea of society-skewering Lenny Bruce when handcuffed
And dragged off stage by the vice squad for the last time,
"Please don't take my words from me!"

The feeding frenzy surrounding Elvis Presley's death
Which prompted a Hollywood agent's sardonic remark,
"Great career move."

The Pale Rider, The Great Motivator, The Journey's End,
The King of Terrors, The Downward Path, The Great Leveler,
The Dreamless Sleep, The Back of Beyond, The 13th Tarot Card,
The Bone that Stammers, The Inevitable Hour, The Ending Days,
Hangin' on to the Drop Edge of Yonder, Hell's Hungry Dog,
The Big Sleep, The Big Downer, The Closed Umbrella,
The Consort to Lady Lust, Life's Interrogator:

Flamboyant figures of speech for the final password,
Rhapsodies on a theme of an Old Norse word,
The hell-for-leather one
Infused with cabalistic power,
Pronounced with a babel
Of accents

Even by the grandfather of dictionaries,
Doctor Johnson (whose conversation Boswell
Described as polished as a second edition),
Who bruited out from his London deathbed,
"*Iam morturrus*" ("I who am about to die"),
The gladiator's final cry.
Or by the more metaphysical Fyodor Dostoevski,
"Did you hear? Hold me not back.
My hour has come. I must die. . . . "

Or the phlegmatic Lord Palmerston,
"Die, my doctor? That's the last thing I'll do."
Or the bilious Alexander Pope,
"Here I am dying of a hundred good symptoms."
Or the nonplussed Thomas Carlyle,
"So, this is death? Well . . . "
Or the nervous Bizet,
"I am in a cold sweat.
It is the sweat of death."

Or the contemptuous Bloomsbury
Biographer extraordinaire Lytton Strachey,
"If this is dying, then I don't think much of it."
Or the resigned novelist Nicholas Gogol,
"I shall have a bitter death."
Or the didactic industrialist Abram Hewitt,
"And now I am officially dead."
Or the heroic Samson,
"Let me die with the Philistines."

Or the repentant Casanova,
"I have lived a philosopher
And am dying a Christian."
Or the tragically misdiagnosed Jane Austen,
When asked if she needed anything,
"Nothing but death."

In the old fable about Frog and Scorpion on the riverbank
The conniving Scorpion asked old innocent Frog
If he could ride across the dangerous water on his back.
Certainly, Frog replied, as long as you promise not to sting me.
In the middle of the torrential river, of course, Scorpion,
Out of sheer instinct, stung Frog, and as the churning waves
Began to overcome them, Frog managed to croak,
"Whyever did you sting me? You're killing us both."
"It's my nature," gasped Scorpion with his dying breath.

✜

There is a deathward swoon,
An apprehension that reaches
Down to the very carbon
In those whose nature it is
To take their own lives,
Leaving behind them
In their clawed pockets,
Gnawed memoirs,
Singed blueprints,
Evidence of the short-circuiting
Of their self-preservation instinct,
Cordite-like clues to self-sabotaging
Through rage-black nights:

A harrowing echo
Of the trumpeter swan
Who wanders onto a drifting ice floe,
Falls asleep in a snowstorm,
Awakens with its orange and black webbed feet
Wedged frozen into the ice,
Its chilling cries
Scratching the air over the tundra
Until its slumbering mate finally hears
The grieving of her blinding white world
As it splits up all around her—
And slowly she lifts her long white neck up
Into a feathered question mark—
And sees
Nothing.

Nothing.
Only a blinding white flash not unlike what Vladimir Mayakovsky
Must have seen as he disappeared into the Siberian desolation,
Leaving behind only a final poem that ended with the words,
". . . the small boat of love is shattered against
The flow of life. I'm through with it.
Useless to dredge up the sorrow,
The sadness . . . the . . . I don't know how to say it . . .
Les torts reciproques . . . Be happy. V. M."

Nothing but inner pandemonium,
As in the soul of Cato the Younger,
Who stoically immolated himself saying,

"Now I am becoming myself."
Or Cleopatra upon seeing the asp in the basket of fruit,
"So here it is."

Or Hannibal who decided on final surrender on his own terms
Rather than being captured by his sworn enemy
By drinking down the poison he always carried with him,
"It's time now to end the great anxiety of the Romans
Who have grown weary of waiting for the death
Of a hated old man . . . ."

Or the corrosively depressed novelist, Virginia Woolf,
Who confessed to her husband in a suicide note
Before walking into the sea with heavy stones in her pocket,
"I feel I am going mad again. I feel we can't go through
Another one of those terrible times. Everything has gone
From me but the certainty of your goodness.
I can't go on spoiling your life . . .
I don't think two people could have
Been happier than we have been . . . ."

Or the despondent actor Paul Bern, after castrating himself,
Writing in his farewell note to his wife, Jean Harlow,
"You understand that last night was only a comedy."
Or the morose poet Vachel Lindsay who wept while
His wife tried in vain to resuscitate him,
"They tried to get me—I got them first.
I just tried to kill myself by drinking Lysol."

Or television news broadcaster Chris Hubback who horrified
Her primetime audience by shooting herself on the air,
"And now, in keeping with Channel 40's policy
Of always bringing you the latest in blood and guts,
In living color you're about to see another first—
An attempted suicide—"

Or actor George Sanders who numbed himself to death,
"Dear World, I am leaving because I'm bored.
I feel I have lived long enough.
I am leaving you with worries
In this sweet cesspool—
Good Luck!"

Or Kodak founder George Eastman
Whose final image was a suicide note,
"To my friends: my work is done. Why wait? G. E."
Or the shadow-haunted photographer Diane Arbus,
Who airbrushed herself away in her last journal entry,
"The last supper."
Or the samurai novelist Yamada Mishima
Who chanted three times before committing seppuku,
"*Tenno Haika Banzai!*" "Long live the Emperor!"

Or the inconsolable Hart Crane after an output
Of one poem during his Guggenheim year in Paris,
Weeping to his wife that he was in disgrace,
Then shouting to his fellow passengers as he leapt off
An oceanliner in his pajamas into the sea,
"Goodbye, everybody, goodbye!"

Or the last screeching riff of Jimi Hendrix,
Which had a two-line lyric with an infinite turnaround,
"The story of love is hello and goodbye. Until we meet again. . . ."
Or the final lacerating cry of Marilyn Monroe,
Who cried out over the phonelines to Peter Lawford,
"Say goodbye to Pat, say goodbye to the President,
And say goodbye to yourself because you're a nice guy."
Or the blacksunspotted poet-publisher Harry Crosby
Who morbidly predicted his suicide in verse,
"My dying words shall be a lover's sighs,
Beyond the last faint rhythms
Of her thighs."

"Australian aborigine shamans say:
God-men say when die go sky
through Pearly Gates where river flow,
God-men say when die we fly
just like eagle-hawk and crows—
might be, might be; but I don't know."

In your garden
A stone is about to explode
As the temperature drops after dark

What pattern does the shattered stone
Create when it falls
Back to the garden?

These soulstorms
Leave us
Thunderstruck

"We only die," wrote Trotsky from Mexico,
"when we fail to take root
in others."

Sometime between the detonation of two shotguns,
The cafés of Montparnasse and the cabins of Minnesota,
Hemingway wrote, "Look, you con man, make a living
Out of your death," then later boasted to a friend,
"It is the inalienable right of man
To go to hell in his own way."

Somewhere along the Marne, Walter Mitty sat calmly
In the cratered foxhole while bullets whirred
Overhead and bombs exploded all around him.
"It's 40 kilometers through hell, sir," said the sergeant.
Mitty finished one last brandy before replying.
"After all," he said coolly,
"what isn't?"

Something must die in you for everything you have learned.
It is lurking like a black alligator
Spying a white heron in a moss-green swamp.

V

The hour of the wolf is near . . .

THE hour of the wolf is near.
Gnarled midnight fog unfurls
Around the amber streetlamps,
While across the glass-sharded street
A silhouetted man hunches over his arching saxophone
Spewing murderous molten blues.
Who is he?

Last night I feverdreamed that I was a young boy again,
Trapped with my rock-ribbed, fear-stilled family
In our 1960 black Ford Falcon as it teetered
On a sheer cliffside, bald tires burning rubber,
Spewing an acrid smell into the knife-edged night air.
I hold my breath so we don't plunge forward—
I hold my screams in so I don't upset the car—
I hold my hands back from grabbing the steering wheel—
I hold my words back—

Until my first words
Threaten to be our last—
"*Can't we back up?*"

Deadweight words
That drop onto the floor
With a dull thud,
Overturning our precipitous balance
And hurtling us . . . screamlessly . . .
Into the lead-colored sea.

I wake up folded into myself, convoluted like a piece
Of jagged brain coral that has broken off a reef
In a terrible squall and fallen to the turbulent sea floor.

Years later I suddenly asked my startled father
As we drove through the landlocked streets of our Michigan hometown,
Where the cliff was where we had almost driven off into the sea.
Only then—as the words surfaced like absurd air bubbles—
Did I realize I had believed in an unvoiced dream for years.
Another needless nightmare believed in for not having been voiced,

Or an uncanny image that resolved
A soul crisis otherwise
Unresolvable?

How does a son tell his father
That he has the third eye,
That he sees invisible things?

How does a man reveal that he has come upon
The secret signs, that he has seen in the falcon's flight
A loved one's soul flying away to the afterworld?

"Life must be understood backwards but lived forwards,"
Admonished Wittgenstein, the metaphysician with his wordbalm
From the land of the midnight sun,
A light not meant
To be stared
Into directly.

> The unnamed can shape us,
> while, with the smoldering madness upon us,
> we shape what we name.

These words are eternity talking in its sleep,
A brother leaning up on one elbow
Speaking sleepstrange words
From deep within the underglimmer
After hearing a sudden *thunderclap*
On a cloudless night.

These words turn the crank handle of the world
By asking the indispensable questions,
The posers that must coil forever,

As the wise ones teach us to phrase
The right questions at the key moments,
That Cheshire Cat-curiosity translates the jabberwocky
Down in the rabbit hole of the human heart,
That last questions are first answers
Turned inside out:

Just ask Gertrude Stein who was pursued on her deathbed
By Alice B. Toklas' desperate interrogation,
"But what is the answer? But what is the answer? But what is the answer?"
Until the Sybil of Montparnasse could only respond rhetorically,
"What is the *answer*? . . . In that case, what is the *question*?"

Or the jesuitical Teilhard de Chardin,
"Why is it I am the only one who sees?"
Or the prolific Cotton Mather who wondered,
"Is this dying? Is this what I feared
When I prayed against a hard death?"
Or the confused Lady Astor,
"Is this death or is it my birthday?"

Or the incredulous Charlotte Brontë,
"I'm not going to die, am I? He will not separate us?"
Or the pyrophobic Voltaire,
"What, the flames already?"
Or the electric shadowmaster John Ford,
"Would you pass me another cigar?"

Or the disappointed Elinor Wylie,
Having a seizure minutes after arranging her poems,
"Is that all it is?"
Or abolitionist Frederick Douglass,
Taken by surprise by the arbitrariness of it all,
"Why, what does this mean?"
Or theater producer Charles Frohman, reassuring friends
As seawater poured through the portholes of the *Lusitania*,
"Why fear death? Death is only a beautiful adventure."

Or naturalist John Burroughs,
"How far are we from home?"
Or the original stoic, Zeno,
"Earth, do you demand me?"
Or Major Norman Baesell to bandleader Glenn Miller

Just before takeoff of their fatal flight over the English Channel,
"What's the matter, Miller, do you want to live forever?"
Or poet-painter Dante Rossetti,
"Do you really think I'm dying? At last you think so.
But I was right first."

Or the religion-crazed poet William Cowper,
"What does it signify?"
Or the fearful, tubercular
Robert Louis Stevenson who implored his wife,
"What's that? Do I look strange?"
Or William Palmer, the 17th-century gentleman
Who cruelly poisoned his best friend,
Then with dark irony asked the hangman about the shaky gallows,
"Are you sure it's safe?"

Or Charles Pierce, a convicted murderer,
"What is the scaffold? A shortcut to heaven."
Or with Louis XIV who mocked his servants,
"Why do you weep? Did you think I was immortal?"
Or Fouquier-Tinville, the dreaded barber of the Revolution,
Exhibiting no gallows humor when beneath the Nation's Razor,
"But *I* am the axe. Am *I* not the axe?"
Or Father John Houghton, hanged, drawn, and quartered
By Henry VIII's executioner, as they ripped his chest apart,
"Good Jesus, what will you do with my heart?"
Or the American football player, Stone Jackson,
Killed on the field after a neck-snapping tackle,
"Oh my God, oh my God! Where's my head? Where's my head?"

Or the Louisiana demagogue Huey Long,
"I wonder why he shot me?"
Or the oblivious, poisoned, and castrated
Mad monk Rasputin, who screamed at his assassins,
"What do you want of me?"
Or the parsimonious Samuel Butler,
"Did you bring the checkbook, Alfred?"
Or the patriotic Thomas Jefferson,
Hoping to die on Independence Day,
"Is this the Fourth?"

Or theater critic Nicholas Boileau
Who lambasted a visiting playwright

Who wanted him to read his play,
"Do you wish to hasten my last hour?"
Or Moe Berg, Red Sox catcher, WWII spy,
And member of the Linguistic Society,
"How did the Mets do today?"
Or the tranquil William Wordsmith,
Murmuring to his wife,
"Is that you, Dora?"
Or Washington Irving,
"When will this end?"

Or the tormented Heisenberg
With quantum questions
Leaping in advance for God,
"Why relativity and why turbulence . . . ?
I really think He may have an answer
To the first question."

Or the skeptical Alexander Dumas,
Who implored his son to assure him,
"Tell me, on your soul and conscience,
Do you believe anything of mine will live?"
Or the skittish Dorothy Parker,
"I want you to tell me the truth.
Did Ernest [Hemingway] really like me?"
Or the satyrical novelist Henry Miller,
"When is this merry-go-round going to stop?"

And the fearless hunter in the Eskimo fairy tale
Who asked brazenly of the howling night,
"Who comes? Is it the hound of death?"

And the death-eater-jawed
Scavenger-eyed poet William Burroughs,
When interviewed about
Life after death,
"How do you know
We're not dead already?"
And the languid novelist Jean Rhys,
When asked why she wrote,
"To earn death?"

And the Chinese philosopher Chuang Tzu,
"Who has forgotten words so
I can have a word with him?"

And the harrower of hell St. Paul,
"Death, where is your victory?
Grave, where is your sting?"

And the Salinas novelist William Saroyan,
To his family after a wire service reporter
Brusquely contacted him for obituary information,
"Everybody has got to die,
But I always believed an exception
Would be made in my case. Now what?"

And the lost little girl inside the Looking Glass,
"The question is whether you can make words
Mean different things."

What is it?
What *is* it?
What it *is*—

Shouted the high-flying
forward after a triple-pumper
basket at the final buzzer

Deadlines:
Lifelines hurled to us
Like life preservers
Of saving grace
To cling to
In the coldcrested sea

Lastlines:
Endpoints
Final questions
Fulgarites smoking like an omen
In the resiny bark
Of the redwood tree

Trilobites of language
Fossilized in the stone of memory
Coelancanths of quotes
Petrified missing links
Sinking deeper into the rockbed
Until I dig them up and reassemble them

Answer them
With the intense heat
Of original questions
That thaws the life
Frozen within me
Like a mammoth
In a remote
Blue
Glacier

Pour plaster into the molds
Of the clinching fingers
Left by lovers in Pompeii bedrooms
As the hot black dust
Fell all
Around them

What would I say if I was in the place
Of the Cambodian prisoner of war
Who was a doctor acting deaf and dumb,
When his North Vietnamese captors asked him
If he could read the medicine bottle
That could save the life of his closest friend?

I pay an eternal price for my nitroglycerine silence.

What would I do if imprisoned in darkness?
Press my eyelids, as Salvador Dali imagined he would,
To release the riot of night vision?
Not an academic question at all.
During the Reign of Terror in France
Prisoners were sealed into coffin-sized stone cells,
Oubliettes, and forgotten until 100 years later

When the grisly tombs were discovered during an underground
Search for new wine vaults, along with
Their last words, which had been scratched
Into the granite walls with their fingernails.
Two centuries later tourist guides
Blithely refer to them as
"Death's graffiti."

Now I press my tongue and speak in livid color.

Night after night for a thousand years
I have haunted the bookstore of transparent
Walls and honeycomb halls, to meet with phantom minds
Who guide me around the deadfalls, through false door after false door,
Then into a burgundy room with carnival mirrors
And a tall spiral ladder, which I climb to reach
A private library to smell the lusty perfume of musty books,
And feel my hand go pneumatically
To a floating shelf and pull down
The deep-breathing manuscript
With sun-faded bindings
And leathery knowledge.

My hands suddenly burn like frostbite
As I touch the embossed Brittany seal
On the crimson cover of the book.
Ancient voices shadow-pierce me with cool
Warnings of my susceptibility
To the venerable words, their two-fold power
Casting a sly spell of beauty
That sometimes blinds me to the living
Words, my own words.

I turn the first page.
The white light engulfs me.
The manuscript crumbles.

I am outside the inside.
I have lost the way
Back.

I feel I could be buried here.

An ivory door appears at the top
Of the hovering ladder
That leads to unknown things.
Open it.
A man hands me a blood-bound book with pages of ice.
Drink it.
It is the dreambook
Of a common
Language.

Breathe deep,
Smell long
The sweet print.

In the labyrinth
Of its sacred verbs
Awaits the secret god.

Close the door behind you.
It may leak
The dark.

VI

Stalking the wild stag through the tunnels
of the twice-black cave, the weary hunter
loses the animal's trail . . .

STALKING the wild stag through the tunnels
Of the twice-black cave, the weary hunter loses
The animal's trail, raises his flaming cresset
Torch and surprises the slumbering bats high
On the dank ceiling of the soaring chamber.
A spark leaps into his heart. He pauses,
Stares at his flickering shadow among theirs,
There where the darkness is divine,
Knows that something ferocious is called for,
The stirring of a god, supernal colors,
An infernal light, a sorcerer's images
Leaping forever across the sanctuary walls:

The dilating of his soul for the mother light,
Not unlike Wolfgang Goethe on his deathbed
40,000 years later, who cried out for
"More light."
Or Teddy Roosevelt who politely asked for less,
"Please turn out the lights."
Or any "Light! All light!"
Like Augustus Bozzi Granville.
Or the flashing strobes of Victor Hugo,
"I see the black light."
Or the mental fireworks of Aldous Huxley
Who asked his wife for an injection of
"LSD—try it intermuscular—100mm—"

Light itself clung to like a lighthouse keeper in a hurricane,
Like a sun-stroked painter at high noon in a blazing cornfield,
Like a war photographer shooting No Man's Land by nightflare,
Like a surgeon amputating by guttering candlelight,
Like a night pilot flying the mail pouches under a blue moon,
Like an astronomer scanning the heavens for the pulsing 10th planet,
Like a submarine captain evading depth charges by green glowing radar.

Light, as final companion, as it was for the shamus
Of short stories, William Sydney Porter,

Who died anonymously of cirrhosis of the liver
With nine empty whiskey bottles under his hospital bed,
After pleading with his nurse, who could not have known
Her patient's *nom de plume* was O. Henry,
"Turn up the lights—
I don't want to go home
In the dark."

And the Irish playwright J. W. Synge
Who asked to be propped up in bed for a final look
At the soft green light over the Dublin hills,
"It's very hard to die knowing
I have so much work left in me."
And the sculptor Saint-Gaudens
Who confessed while roaming into the gloaming,
"It's very beautiful,
But I want to go farther away."
And the philosopher Frederick Humboldt who exclaimed,
"How grand these rays!
They seem to beckon earth to heaven!"

And the recluse Jean-Jacques Rousseau who admitted,
"I go to see the sun for the last time."
Or Charles II of France whose last regal request was,
"Open up the curtains so that I can once more see day."
Or the German educator Friedrich Froebel who demanded
A final dalliance with the outdoors,
"My friend, I have peeked at lovely Nature all my life.
Permit me to pass my last hours
With this enchanting mistress."

Or Colette who pointed out to her husband
The summer swallows as they passed her window,
"Maurice, look, look!"
Or novelist Francis Marion Crawford who sighed as she died,
"I love to see the reflection of the sun on the bookcase."
Or the Napoleonic court painter Jean-Jacques David,
Examining a print of his own work as he expired,
"Too dark . . . too light . . . the dimming of the light
Is not well enough indicated . . . this place is blurred,
However, I must admit, that is a unique head of Leonidas. . . ."

Or Jean-Baptiste Corot, hallucinating as he stared
At the blank canvas of ceiling in his room,
"How beautiful it is! I have never seen such beautiful landscapes."
Or the American John Dekker, remarking on his hospital flowers,
"The blossoms are of the same color Raphael used."
Or the landscapist Thomas Gainsborough,
"We are going to heaven, and Van Dyck is of the company."
Or the Japanese painter Hokusai,
"If Heaven had only granted me five more years!"

Or Paul Cézanne, whose color-divining hand
Death stilled mid-stroke on a lightning-jolted country road,
And who died hours later while remembering the name
Of the Director of the Museum at Aix-en-Provence
Who had once refused to exhibit his luminous paintings,
"Pointier! Pointier!"

Or Georges Clemenceau at the cemetery in Giverny
While draping the coffin of his friend Claude Monet,
"He would have liked the splash of *red*."

If not sight then sound
When nature calls in her debt,
Music, the anti-word, the aural dance,
Reverberating cathedrals of sound
In the inner ear as the baton drops,
And we hear the final fugue
Roll in on wave after wave
After wave,

As for the Sufi poet Mirabeau who murmured,
"Let me fall asleep to the sound of delicious music."
Or the ornithologist Alexander Wilson who wished,
"Bury me where the birds will sing over my grave."
Or the German mystic Jacob Boehme who predicted,
"Do you hear the music? Now I go hence."
Or the children's author Mary-Anne Schimmelpennick who exclaimed,
"Oh, I hear such beautiful voices, and the children are the loudest."
Or the visionary William Blake who reassured his wife

About the alleluias he was singing on his deathbed,
"My beloved, they are not mine, no, they are not mine."

Or Frederick Chopin whose last thoughts were of the master,
"Play Mozart in memory of me."
Or Gustav Mahler who echoed the homage,
"Little Mozart, little Mozart."
Or Wolfgang Amadeus, who reminded his wife,
"Did I not tell you I was writing the 'Requiem' for myself?"
Or Franz Schubert who insisted,
"No, it is not true, Beethoven does not lie here."
Or Ludwig himself, even after taking fate by the throat,
As thunder and lightning crashed—silently to his ears—
"Pity, pity . . . it's too late . . . I shall hear in heaven."
Or the indefatigable Enrico Caruso,
"I am unable to get my breath!"

Or for the philosopher Friedrich Nietzsche,
Who finally forgave Richard Wagner
From his sanitarium deathbed,
"Him I loved much."
Or the madman of Bayreuth himself,
"I am fond of them, the inferior beings
Of the abyss, of those who are full of longing."
Or the gangrenous Scriabin rationalizing that
"Suffering is necessary."
Or the grateful Tchaikovsky acknowledging his patron,
"Nadejda."
Or the dissonant Schoenberg suddenly remembering,
"Harmony."
Or Mendelsohn,
"Weary, very weary."
Or Mussorgsky,
"It's the end. Woe is me."
Or Liszt,
"Tristan!"

Or the romanticizer of the struggling artist, Henry Murger,
"No music, no noise, no Bohemia."
Or the consummate cabaret Bohemian, Edith Piaf,
"I can die now; I've lived twice."
Or Louis Armstrong on the night before he died,
Scatting with his agent after being devastated

By the panning of his last gig by a two-bit critic,
"Are you still gonna book me, Joe?"
Or barrelhousing jazz pianist Fats Waller,
Shivering to death on a cold sleeper car
While the wind howled wildly outside,
Imagining he heard his old sax sideman,
"Yeah, Hawkins is sure blowing out there tonight."
Or blues-bedevilled Huddie Ledbetter,
Alias Leadbelly, vamping his doctor,
"If I put this here guitar down, I ain't ever gonna wake up."
Or Louis de Lisle, New Orleans' legendary clarinetist,
"The blues? Ain't no first blues. The blues always been.
Blues is what cause the fellow to start jazzin'."

Or essayist John Jay Chapman,
Plucking on his wife's fingers like a harp,
"No, the mute, the mute. I want to play on the open strings."
Or composer Ralph Vaughn Williams,
In an interview two weeks before his death,
"If I were reincarnated . . . I would like to be a landscape painter
But in the next world I shan't be doing music . . .
With all the strivings and disappointments . . .
I shall be *being* it. . . ."

Then again, as many of the ancients predicted,
Ambrosia and nectar have been called for
Just as the underworld journey was under way,
As for the famished Russian director
Nicholas Rubenstein, dying in the arms of Turgenev,
"Oysters! Nothing will do me so much good
As a dozen oysters and an ice afterwards!"
Or the Duc de Lunzon, asking his chaperone to the tumbrils,
"I beg a thousand pardons, my friend, but permit me
To finish this last dozen oysters."
Or the smirking comedian Lou Costello,
Delivering one last comeback to his pal Bud Abbot,
"That was the best ice cream I ever tasted."
Or F. Scott Fitzgerald scribbling to Sheila Graham
In the margin of his last article,
"I'm going to Schwabs for an ice cream. . . ."

Or dreamweaver psychologist Carl Jung,
Who turned away visitors in his final days saying,
"No more people . . . I'm preparing to die,"
Then died peacefully after asking,
"Let's have a really fine red wine tonight."
Or Russian playwright Anton Chekov
Who had a final drink on his doctor's orders,
"I haven't had champagne for ages."
Or Johannes Brahms, whose final lullaby
Was a hearty glass of wine,
"Ah, that tastes nice, thank you."
Or Marcel Proust, whose last privileged moment
Was an icy beer in his cork-lined room,
"Mother. . . ."

Or Tallulah Bankhead, mashing her last lines
As an order to her nurse to bring her
"Bourbon. . . ."
Or the last of the Irish bards, Turlough Carolan,
Unable to swallow his native whiskey,
"It would be hard if two such friends
Should part without kissing."
Or physicist James Croll,
Calculating a final drop of Scotch,
"I'll take a wee drop o' that.
I don't think there's much fear o' me
Learning to drink now."
Or bibulous W. C. Fields,
Swearing off a final shot,
"I've drunk to so many other people's health
I have none left of my own."

Or the English painter J. W. Turner,
Who abdicated his final drink to his doctor,
"Go downstairs. Take a glass of sherry
Then look in on me again . . . well, I suppose
I am a nonentity now. . .
The sun is God."

Or "Bood" Boudinet Crumpton, the Western outlaw
Sent to the gallows for murder while on a drunken spree,
Who pointed to the hangman's noose around his neck,

"Men, the next time you lift a glass of whiskey,
I want you to look into the bottom of the glass and see
If there isn't a hangman's noose in it like the one here."
Or fellow murderer Neville Heath's last request for whiskey,
"Ah, you might make that a double."
Or science-fiction writer Jaroslat Hasek,
Objecting to his doctor's refusal of a final brandy,
"But you're cheating me!"

Or the irascible Welsh poet Dylan Thomas
After a late-night binge boasting to his wife,
"I've just had 18 straight whiskies, I think that's the record";
Then waking up in bed to rage, rage, rage
Against his own dying light,
"I love you but I am alone. . . ."

The sky crackles
I feel a catch-in-the-breath
As the smell of the storm passes by

There are runes
Within the ruins
Read them

Read the words of the world
That have the fire of the firefly in the lantern
The kick of the martial arts master

The ones that crash
Like the horns of clashing buffaloes
Shrouded in fistthickfog

Ones pressed into the mysterious book
Held against your bruised heart
In the wisdom dream

About the jousting knight
Whose spear hurled into your chest
Is blunted by the birch-bark cover

Muir Beach glimmers under starlight
Like the pearls of a young girl's necklace.
I pace on wave-slapped shores
Memorizing passages
From Rexroth's "Dragon and Unicorn."
Gradually my thoughts return homeward,
His lilting words crackling over the long-distance
Lines like a baseball announcer's voice
Coming through a young boy's crystal radio,

"It's later than you think, son;
So remember Orwell's last words:
'At 50 we all have the face we deserve!'"

The tang of things
The arcane edge
The *aarrgghh* in the bass note
The middle of the riddle
The commotion in the emotion
The tremolo in the piano
The exultation in imagination

Visions made visible
By the alone
For the alone

Since
To *find* is the thing
The thing-in-itself

The hidden thing that moves
The sun and the stars,
The 10,000 things

The very stuff
To go through
For the strange change

As once
Early mapmakers
Were inspired rather than terrified
By the vast uncharted seas
Calling the lands-yet-to-be-found
"Sleeping beauties,"
Princesses longing to be discovered
Behind the brambled mist
Of their long slumber

"I don't search, I find,"
bellowed the minotaur
to the coy goddess
holding up the mirror
showing me

I am forever
going
home

VII

And now the conquistador tilts his lance
and charges the churning windmills
because they might be giants

CRAWLING for centuries through a long chambered tunnel
That winds on into itself like a nautilus shell,
I emerge into dazzling light only to have to climb for eons more
Up the rune-rhymed keys of a Cheops pyramid-sized typewriter,
Where a wily dragon grins and blows clouds of hot ink in my face
That I wipe off with a hand which dissolves into smoke.
A droll troll of a cartoonist nods knowingly
Atop the typewriter carriage that rat-a-tat-chets along
As I step from key to key typing out my last words
Until a baffling one-liner in balloon dialogue
Rises above us in hilarious italics:

"*God did not use footnotes either.*"

Nor does the gloomy ferryman on the river Styx,
Even for those bamboozled by fate,
Hornswaggled by destiny,
Snookered by kismet,
Flabbergasted by the weird sisters,
Steamrollered by fortune's wheel,

Or blindsided by hubris
Like the archetypal mathematician Archimedes
Who persisted on drawing a last diagram in the sand
After being arrested by a humorless centurion,
Then was rudely interrupted by a dagger while saying,
"Don't step on my circle, you're spoiling it—"

And the unsuspecting Civil War General John Sedgewick,
High in the spurs, roaring above crossfire,
"Why, they couldn't hit an elephant at this dist—"
And Captain Bucky O'Neil of the Rough Riders,
Whose boasting to his troops was cut short,
"Don't worry, Sergeant, the Spanish bullet

Isn't molded that will kill me—"
And Oregon cowboy Hiram Gulch shaking his fist at the sky,
"If I ever rustled a cow, may the Good Lord strike me dead—"

And Guiseppe Zangara, assassin of Chicago mayor Anton Cermak,
After an initial sentence of 80 years hard labor,
Sent to the electric chair after challenging his judge,
"Don't be stingy, give me 100 years—"
And Captain Aristide Dupetit-Thouars,
French naval commander in the 1798 Franco-Russian war,
His legs blown off by cannonfire, perched upright
In a barrel on his bleeding stumps so he could scream orders
As the fighting raged on, until so riddled with wounds, he cried,
"I might lose my head with my blood
And do something foolish
If I keep the command—"

And Wild Bill Hickok, while holding those Eights and Aces,
The Dead Man's Hand, in Deadwood, South Dakota,
Shot in the back after scoffing at the idea of changing seats,
"The old duffer—he broke me on the last hand—"
And Anthony J. Drexel III, an 1890s financier,
Showing off his infamous gun collection,
"Here's one you've never seen before—"
And Blackbeard the pirate toasting a rival captain,
"Damnation seize my soul if I give you any quarter
Or take any from you—"
And Captain Cook, cannibalized after his retreat was cut short,
"Take to the boats—"

And Carl "Alfalfa" Switzer from "Our Gang,"
Gunned down while drunkenly arguing in a bar,
"I want the 50 bucks you owe me and I want it now—"
And French encyclopedist Denis Diderot,
Who harrumphed during a last bite into a poisonous apricot,
"How in the devil can it hurt me?"
And Daniel Webster,
Who should have defined his terms better,
"I still live—"

And swaggering James Dean shouting to a young German friend
Above the engine roar of his candy-apple red Porsche

While hurtling towards his final stop sign,
Martyrdom and immortality,
"That guy up there's got to stop;
He'll see us—"

And the chartreuse danseuse Isadora Duncan,
As she drove off in her gleaming white Dusenberg,
"I go off to glory—*adieu*—"

And basketball wizard Pistol Pete Maravich
Who collapsed at courtside one afternoon not knowing
He had been playing in sudden death overtime
All his life with an oversized heart,
"I really feel great . . .
I should do this more often—"

And the Cherokee Kid, the irrepressible Will Rogers,
Who was writing his weekly column over Barrow, Alaska,
When his plane ran out of gas, the mangled typewriter
Found in the wreckage later with the keys
Frozen mid-strike above the "h" in
"death."

If not for the whims of impetuous fate,
What about the brassy chorus of irony
Gloating over the sudden collapse of Ivan the Terrible
Onto his chessboard after boasting to his court
That his doctors were dead wrong,
"According to the soothsayers,
Today is the day I should draw my last breath;
But I feel my strength reviving.
So let the impostors prepare for death—"

And Henri Beyle, aka Stendahl, who grumbled
A few months before being felled by a stroke
On the cobblestone streets of Paris,
"I find that there is nothing ridiculous
About dying in the street,
Provided one does not do it deliberately."

And Albert Camus who was killed in a car crash
Hours after joking morbidly to the wife
Of his best friend that should he and his friend
Die before her she should place their corpses
In her living room to ensure
That she would never forget them.

And young cancer-stricken football player Brian Piccollo,
Falling into a coma after shrieking to his wife,
"I'm going to lick this . . .
I'm going to get out of here . . .
Can you believe it, Joy . . .
Can you believe this shit . . . ?"

And film critic and novelist James Agee,
Vowing at a posh party at Gloria Vanderbilt's,
To finish his novel *A Death in the Family*,
Then dying in a taxicab on his way home.
And civil rights activist, and preacher,
Martin Luther King, Jr., confiding to Jesse Jackson
Moments before his final speech was to begin,
"Be sure to sing 'Precious Lord Take My Hand.'
Be sure to sing it pretty."

And Jerome Kern who died on a New York street corner
In the arms of Oscar Hammerstein who softly sang him
A last chorus of "Old Man River."
And country crooner Hank Williams who passed away
In a Cadillac taxicab hours after recording
"I'll Never Get Out of Here Alive."
And mobster Jack Zuta who was shot down by Al Capone's men
While the café jukebox played
"Good for You, Bad for Me."
And rocker Buddy Holly who died in a plane crash,
While his latest song climbed the charts,
"It Doesn't Matter Anymore."
And whiskey-veined Janis Joplin
Who overdosed after listening to her own recording
Of "Buried Alive in the Blues."

And war photographer Robert Capa,
Whose most vivid dream was unemployment,

A man who invented himself, a human metaphor
For the 20th-century nauseated, existential hero
Paratrooping behind enemy lines
With a warrior's courage,
A bodhisattva's smile, a madman's folly,
Until his deadline came on a landmine in Vietnam
Moments after clicking a few last shutters
And drawling to his comrades,
"I'm going up the road a little bit.
Look for me when you get started again."

In moments of soul deadlock
I slowly turn the iron dial
Listening for velvet tumblers to click

In that corner of night
That razors through
The blueblack grief
In that *one true sentence*
Someone daringly confides in me
I boldly reveal to another

Light pours into my heart like radiant sunshafts
Streaming through the rose window
At Chartres cathedral

And I see the great consolation,
And I hear the great conversation,
And I feel the secret of secrets

Moving closer and closer—

And the haunted ink bottle cries out,
"He who lives more lives than one
More deaths than one must die"

And the signature reappears,
"Who dies not before he dies
Is ruined before he dies"

And there is a spiraling
Inward to the dark center
That hears the song of Orpheus
It is the path downward
The road homeward
To rescue love from death
If only   I don't let go
Of the beloved hand.

> And now the conquistador
> Tilts his lance and charges
> The churning windmills
>
> Because they might be giants

From the top tier
Of the theater at Epidaurus
The muse-intoxicated dramatist
Listens closely to the heartbeat of the world
And his wonder reverberates
For centuries:

> "Life may be death,
> Death may be life.
> Who knows?"

VIII

"I can't afford to die; I have too many deadlines"

FOLLOWING the lead of the Tibetan monks
Who meditate in graveyards as a reminder of mortality,
I pull the Yamaha 850 off the desert highway
Into Tombstone, Texas, and glide past wooden sidewalks
And up to Boot Hill Cemetery, and there, among the white crosses
Is a lopsided gravestone the color of bones:

> Be what you is
> Cuz if you be what you ain't
> Then you ain't what you is

Buried for four thousand years in a pharoah's tomb
In the Valley of the Kings was the papyrus *Book of the Dead*,
With scenes of the Egyptian last judgment revealing the golden scales of Maat
And the weighing of the heart by the jackal-headed god Anubis:
If heavier than a feather the soul of the deceased
Would be dropped into the jaws of the all-devouring crocodile god,
Swallower of the Dead, to be gnawed on for all of eternity.

For the ancient Celts, a warrior's last words
Had to be humorous—the only divine attribute,
The sages decreed—to gain passage to the Otherworld.
Centuries later, on an old wall in Dublin's O'Donoghue's pub,
The itinerant philosopher strikes again
In smoky blue swirling ink,

> "Eternity's a terrible thought; I mean,
> Where's it all going to end?"

Under the Sword of Damocles,
Feeling the heat of the blade,

Hearing the long snake moanin'
On the edge of the cruel radiance,
Some fast-fading souls are still lucid enough
To put the *kibosh*, the cap of death,
Over the great dragon doubt
So they might fleece the golden words,
Verbally dance like Daumier's pencil
Sketching his waltzing skeletons,
Whimsically play with their last moments like Saint-Saëns
With his rattling bone xylophones in the Danse Macabre,

Until they're compelled, like film critic Wilson Mizner,
To break the somber spell with extreme unction to their priest,
"I want a priest, a Protestant minister and a rabbi
To hedge my bets . . . why should I talk to you,
I've just been talking to your boss."
And the Shropshire Lad A. E. Houseman,
Grinning to his doctor after hearing a dirty story,
"Yes, that's a good one, and tomorrow
I'll be telling it again on the Golden Floor."

And one of Dublin's seven deadly sins, Brendan Behan,
Who blustered to the nun caring for him,
"Thank you sister, may you be the mother of a bishop."
And bedridden poet Kenneth Patchen,
Who joked to his best friend and editor,
"Laughlin, when you find out which came first,
The chicken or the egg, you write and tell me."
And the Comtesse of Vercelles
Who broke wind till the bitter end,
"Good! A woman who can fart is not dead!"
And William Henry Vanderbilt,
Worth two hundred million at last count,
"I have had no more real gratification or enjoyment
Than my neighbor on the next block
Who is worth only half a million."

And King Farouk of Egypt,
"There will soon be only five Kings left:
The Kings of England, Diamonds, Hearts, Spades and Clubs."
And Pope Alexander VI,
"This month is deadly for fat people."
And the incorrigible murderer James Rodgers,

When asked if he had a last request,
"Why, yes—a bullet-proof vest."
And the gypsy thief's last wish on the scaffold in Paris,
"A leg of mutton and a woman."
And the Scottish peasant poet James Hogg,
"It is a reproach to the faculty
That they cannot cure the hiccups!"

And the decadent French poet Paul Verlaine
Who chided those who found him in Bohemia's ivory gutter,
"Don't sole the dead man's shoes yet."
And the Divine Sarah Bernhardt who got her revenge on the paparazzi,
"All my life reporters have tormented me enough.
I can tease them a little by making them cool their heels."

And Florenz Ziegfeld after his delirious final curtain,
"Curtain! Fast music! Lights! Ready for the last finale?
Great! The show looks good! The show looks good!"

And Stan Laurel, whose last slapstick routine was for his nurse,
"I wish I was skiing now . . . better to be doing that
Than having all these needles stuck into me!"

"It's not that I'm afraid to die," decrees Woody Allen,
The court jester on the throne of his movie kingdom,
"I just don't want to be there when it happens."

I hold up to my mind's eye
The conic mirror, the anamorphoscope,
Curved glass for gazing into the sunburst of death,
Reassembling my fragmented reflections,
Sharpening the focus on disturbing images,
Vying for a moment's perspective
On the random jumble
Of puzzling lives,
The peculiar acrostics,
The central struggle,
And then at the core of the hurricane
Find the exhilaration
Of black humor,

Daredevil last-act
Improvisations,

Like the wily Edgar Rice Burroughs,
"It's a jungle out there."
Or the earnestly important Oscar Wilde,
"I'm dying as I have lived—beyond my means."
Or the master of malaprop Sam Goldwyn,
"I never thought I'd live to see the day."
Or British Prime Minister Viscount Palmerston,
"Die? That's the last thing I shall do."
Or Elisa Bonaparte when told nothing was certain as death,
"Except taxes."
Or Benjamin Franklin who coined
Poor man aphorisms to the very end,
"A dying man can do nothing easy."
Or the versatile Lionel Barrymore,
"I've played everything but the harp."
Or John Huston, directing right to the final shot
When he advised his actress daughter,
"Knock 'em dead, honey!"

Or Thomas Lovell Beddoes, author of *Death's Jest Book*,
"I am food for what I am good for—worms."
Or Civil War hero General Lewis Armistead,
"Give them the cold steel, men."
Or journalist Arthur Brisbane,
"This is the best of all possible worlds."
Or the politically expedient Machiavelli,
"I desire to go to hell and not to heaven. In the former
Place I shall enjoy the company of Popes, Kings and Princes,
While in the latter are only beggars, monks and apostles."
Or the explorer and naturalist John Muir,
"I have led a bully life. I have done what I set out to do."
Or the 19th-century baseball player King Kelly,
Grinning behind his handlebar mustache,
"This is my last slide."

Or the locomotive engineer Casey Jones,
"For I'm going to run her till she leaves the rail—
Or make it on time with the southbound mail."
Or the American humorist Joel Harris,
When asked if he was feeling any better,

". . . about the extent of a tenth
Of a gnat's eyebrow better."
Or the wizardly L. Frank Baum,
"Now we can cross the shifting sands."
Or the absurdist anarchist Alfred Jarry,
"*Je cherche, je cherche. . . .*"
("I search, I search. . . .")

Or Nero,
"What an artist the world is losing in me."
Or Vespasian,
"Well, I suppose I am becoming a god now."
Or Captain Kidd,
"This is a faithless and fickle generation."

Or Henry David Thoreau,
"Moose . . . Indian!"
Or Anna Pavlova,
"Get my swan costume ready!"
Or James Audubon,
"Billy, Billy . . . ducks, ducks . . ."
Or Ulysses S. Grant,
"The fact is I think I am a verb . . ."
Or Dutch Schultz,
"I don't know who shot me . . . French Canadian bean soup. . . ."

Then the sly fool behind the fish-eye lens adds,
"I do not want to achieve immortality through my work,
I want to achieve it through not dying!"

To damn the blank page is the thing,
To find your tongue in the great mouth—
To gear a response to the gravitational pull of infinity,
To satisfy the insatiable urge to create something
To show that we were here and heard the hoofbeats,
To hang on to every second of the creeping hands of time

Like the timebender comic Harold Lloyd
On the clocktower in *The College Boy*,

Just long enough to deliver one last line,
(Believing along with John Donne that
"Death is an ascension
To a better library,")

Like Heinrich (Never Say Die) Heine who glibly told friends,
"God will pardon me: it's his profession . . .
Write! Write! Paper! Pencil!"
Or Nicholas Gogol who vowed to Tolstoy he could rewrite his
Dead Souls manuscript after he had burned it in a tirade,
"Yes, yes, I can!"
Or E. A. Robinson who confided
To his bedside editor,
"I shall have more to say when I'm dead."
Or the grammar-obsessed Dominique Bouhours,
"I am about to die—I am going to die:
Either expression is correct."

Or the steadfast novelist Thomas Lovelock
Howling as fire swept his library,
"By the immortal gods, I will not move!"
Or Sydney Smith, the 18th-century English wit,
Told he had drunk ink by mistake,
"Then bring me all the blotting paper there is in the house."
Or Edith Hamilton, the maven of mythology,
"You know, I haven't felt much like writing.
But now I think I am going to finish that book on Plato."
Or the placid Dr. William Hunter,
"If I had the strength to hold a pen,
I would write down how easy and pleasant
A thing it is to die."
Or Herbert Coleridge, an early editor of the *Oxford Dictionary*,
"I must begin Sanskrit tomorrow."

Or British Prime Minister William Gladstone,
From the last entry of his seventy-year diary,
"I do not enter any interior matters. It is so easy
To write, but to write honestly is nearly impossible."
Or Robert Frost in his last journal entry,
"Metaphor is the thing. And poetry is the result."
Or the unassured composer Maurice Ravel,
"Tell me not everything I wrote was bad."
Or the fascist playwright Luigi Pirandello,

"No need to be scared of words, doctor."
And the credit-conscious screenwriter Herman Mankiewicz,
"Well, that finishes everything I've got to take care of
Before I go to meet my maker. Or should I say my co-maker?"
Or the scholar John Raymond,
"How easy to glide from the work here to the work there."

Or Epicurus,
"Now remember
All my words!"

"Do you have any famous last words yet, son?"
"Not yet."
"Are those famous?"

The archaeologist sifts carefully through the sand
Around his startling discovery, calmly, without expectation,
Moving from a notion beyond himself, until just before dusk
He discovers the missing shard, the beguiling image:
The sage's reply to Gilgamesh:

"That which you *seek* you will never find."

Because wherever you are awake
Is the entry
Point

There where the powder monkey finally masters the trick
Of how to turn blood into icewater
While setting the dynamite fuse:
He becomes immovably centered,
Stiller yet than the thing staring at him
From inside the space between the black powder
And the flame:
A tremble,
A sneer,

A spark of doubt
And he will implode
Before the thing he must explode.

And now there is a calm
Before the end
As there was

In the beginning,
As there is
In the palm
Of a sleeping
Child's
Hand.

The final calm, the gentle peace, the Great Death,
As there was for explorer Captain Oates of Scott's
Expedition to the South Pole, who gambled that his friends
Might survive if there were one less man to feed,
Saying to them before he walked into the long white silence,
"I'm going outside . . . and I may be some time. . . ."

And Amelia Earhart in her letter left behind for her husband,
"Please know I am aware of the hazards . . .
I want to do it . . . Women must try to do things as men
Have tried . . . their failures must be a challenge to others. . . ."

And sportswriter Damon Runyan in his last letter,
"You can keep your things of bronze and stone,
And give me one man to remember me once a year."
And songster Stephen Foster scratching in a notebook
Found along with 38 cents in his Bowery apartment,
"Dear friends and gentle hearts."

And the diehard physicist Sir Isaac Newton . . .
"But as to myself . . . I seem to have been only a boy . . .
Playing on the seashore . . . and diverting myself now . . .
And then . . . finding a smoother pebble . . . or prettier shell
Than ordinary . . . whilst the great ocean of truth . . .
Lay all undiscovered . . . before me. . . ."

And Crowfoot, the Blackfoot warrior,
"A little while and I will be gone

From among you, whither I cannot tell.
From nowhere we come, into nowhere we go.
What is life?
It is a flash of a firefly in the night.
It is the breath of the buffalo in the wintertime.
It is the little shadow that runs across
The grass and loses itself in the sunset."

Or the great Russian witness Leo Tolstoy,
Dying on the stationmaster's couch
While confiding to his son, Sergey,
"Come closer . . . it's so simple . . . to seek,
Always to seek . . . I must escape . . .
I love truth very much. . . ."

Or Saint Theresa,
Writhing in death ecstasy,
"Over my spirit flash and float
In divine radiancy the bright
And glorious visions of the world
To which I go."
Or the Mogul emperor Aurungzebe,
"No one has seen the departure of his own soul,
But I know mine is departing."

Or the Dominican philosopher Giordano Bruno,
"I die a martyr and willingly.
My soul shall mount up with the smoke to paradise."
Or the painter Joshua Reynolds,
"I know all good things must come to an end,
And now I have come to mine."
Or Zachary Taylor,
"I regret nothing,
Except leaving my friends."
Or John Quincy Adams,
"This is the last of earth.
I am content."

Or the explorer Henry Stanley,
Expiring, as the legend goes, as Big Ben struck,
"I want to go into the woods to be free . . .
I want to go home . . . How strange.
So that is the time—"

Or the English surgeon Joseph Green who expired
Moments after taking his last pulse—his own—
"Congestion . . .
Stopped."
Or the British divine Edward Hobbes,
Who died fifty-nine minutes after predicting,
"An hour hence I shall depart."
Or the philosopher Ludwig Wittgenstein,
"Tell them I had a wonderful life!"
Or the actress Ethel Barrymore,
"Is everybody happy?
I want everybody to be happy.
I know I'm happy."
Or the poet Gerard Manley Hopkins,
Proclaiming after his deathbed conversion,
"I'm happy! I'm happy! I'm happy!"
Or the indomitable Franz Haydn,
"Cheer up, children, I'm alright."
Or the inventor John Erickson,
"This rest is more magnificent, more beautiful than words can tell."
Or Maud Gonne, the Irish firebrand,
"I feel an ineffable joy."
Or the aspiring art student Iyan Hughes
Who beamed to her landlord her first night in San Francisco,
"I came here to be famous."

Or Benito Aquino to his brother
Moments before deplaning in Manila,
"I can die now."
Or Captain William Smith of the Titanic
As he pushed away the overloaded lifeboat,
"Let me go."
Or the Oglala Sioux warrior Crazy Horse,
"This is a good day to die!"
Or Ishi, the Last Yahi,
"You stay, I go."
Or the Sufi mystic, Mevlana Rumi,
"Do not search for me in the grave.
Look for me in the hearts of men."
Or Meher Baba 44 years *before* he died,
"Don't worry . . . be happy. . . ."
Or Confucius,

"Now it is time to die."
Or Ramakrishna,
"I spit out the body."
Or the prophet Mohammed,
"Oh, Allah, let it be so."
Or the Buddha,
"All that is created must perish. Never cease to struggle."
Or Jesus of Nazareth,
"It is finished."

Or William Thackeray,
"And my heart throbbed with an exquisite bliss."
Or Henry James,
"So, here it is, the distinguished thing."
Or Katherine Mansfield,
"I love the rain. I want to feel it on my face."
Or St. John of the Cross,
"It is time for matins."
Or Emily Dickinson,
"I must go in, for the fog is rising."
Or D. H. Lawrence,
"I am better now."
Or Immanuel Kant,
"It is well."

Or Cyrano de Bergerac,
"Panache."
Or Elizabeth Barrett Browning,
"Beautiful. . . ."
Or Heloise,
"Abelard. . . ."
Or Mahatma Gandhi,
"Ram."
Or Soen Roshi,
"Dream."

"When the Angel of Death approaches, he is terrible,"
Reads the old Muslim text, "when he reaches you
It is bliss."

✣

Joe Two Trees, the Last Algonquin, believed that
As long as one person could still tell the story
Of his people the Old Ones would live on.
One winter night on the banks of the Hudson River
He befriended a 12-year-old boy for The Telling,
That he might die in peace, which he did
After ending his tale with his eyes transfixed
On the sacred centering fire, saying serenely,
"My fate, those things to be, will happen here."

The American anthropologist Alfred Kroeber,
Felled by a sudden stroke while on holiday in Paris,
Drifted in and out of reverie as his wife Theodora
Wove soul-centering stories
Through the rainy night because he had asked her to,
"Tell us about us—from the beginning."

"Thus the flickering frightening
moment passed for us," she later wrote
of his gentle dying at dawn.

"There is a mystery everywhere,"
Types the sportswriter in the pressbox
High above Tiger Stadium's jade green baseball diamond.

It is hiding like a scorpion in a stone quarry,
Glimmering like silver light on blue coral,
Magnetized like the memory palaces of classical orators,

Creaking like the oak chair of your grandmother
That is kept down in the coal cellar
And is heard rocking on certain unpredictable nights.

One drizzly Paris morning
The sculptor with the marble-dusted beard
Feels the new form keening in his fingers,
The soulful thrust within stone conforming
To the Burghers of Calais bold offer to sacrifice
Themselves to save their town.

Rodin eliminates the pedestal on which statues
Had always stood and brings the brooding figures
Down to earth so we might see the face a man puts on
To face death as an equal.

By chiseling the first anti-heroes,
He turns the noble prisoners of war
Into something recognizably human,
And with that ends
The *rigor artis*
Of centuries of sculpture.

The first four burghers are sculpted defiantly enough
To damn the rush of the king's breath
Until he realizes their disdain for execution,
But it is Eustache, the fifth, the leader,
Whose hollowed-in features catch your attention,
His knees slightly bent to slow down
The inexorable march to the royal tent,
His eyes molded to meet the eyes and conscience
Of the pregnant queen, who, he knows,

Carrying life within her womb,
Is closer to the pulse of the world
Than her warrior-king husband,
Who, it is true, she conquers
With the squeeze of a velvet-gloved hand,
And so can grant freedom to the death-defiers.

I sit before inexhaustible images
Of whirling dervish
Transformed grief.

Perhaps it *was* under my eyelids all along.
But it has been my way to line up words
Like Muybridge his cameras along the path
Of galloping horses
To capture the dark movement,
Subdue the shades.

I learn so slowly.
I resist the light so long.
I lose touch with the velvet-gloved hand too often.

Now when I close my eyes
I see myself in soft Mediterranean light
Chiseling words into the keystone
Above the entrance to the dream temples,
Savored lines grounded in the eternals
That the soul healing begins here.

How do I remember them when awake?
How do I pronounce them?
How do I seal the lips of darkness?

You who ask me how much words weigh,
You who remind me every night at half-past fear,
You who push me beyond words,
You who linger on in me
Like Gregorian chant in a nine-domed cathedral,
Tranquilize me with the thrust of your warm tongue in my ear,
Turn my head toward the stenciled logo
On the crumbling walls of the old café along the Seine
I would have walked by again.
And my heart thrums once more like the arrow
Piercing the black and red target as I read:
"*N'oubliez pas l'amour*."

It is then again I remember
The enchanted words,
The words lost in every age,
The words lost every moment,
The words lost in the marginalia
Of that big black book, *Ulysses*, for 50 years,
But rediscovered by wordsleuth scholars
And reinserted into a new edition of my own psychodyssey:

"*Love, the word known to all men*."

Your arms lift like heatwaves
as you come softly to me
with the grace, with the ardor,
with a light that gives me
the strength to pivot,
to turn, to face the one
who walks beside me,
knowing better,
the one who
would breathe in
your dying
breath.

Every embrace with you
is a winepress of emotion
that squeezes darkness
out of me,
and sets sail
the ship
of death.

I was waiting for you.

IX

The shrouded night was long and full of marvels

THE oldest stories we have were once told
To bite off a piece of the dark winter night,
Tales told by those gifted with the magic
Of the vitalizing words: immortal verses
For mortal hearts, tales retold down through the ages
On the knees of glint-in-the-eye grandparents

With words that whistle by the graveyard,
Bend the bars of the prisonhouse of words,
Insist upon the *quickening* of the pulse,
In a language that moves, that rustles
On the page, off the tongue, around the edges of the mind,
Like the oscillating cube of the psychologist's lab
Or the alternating staircases in an Escher print,
Words that leap out in bas-relief to themselves,
Revealing exuberantly the background,

The signature of all things.

For the fury of the hidden wisdom
I read on, for the love of the *jolt*
I gather stories
Like friends on a raft
Careening down a mighty river
Toward a cascading waterfall,

Despite Karl Marx's cantankerous warning,
"Go on, get out, last words are for fools
Who haven't said enough."

And regardless of the deadbeat tale of Holy Goof hipster
Neil Cassady's collapsing on the "64,928th" railroad tie
From a Mexican shantytown—hence his legendary last words.

And taking to heart the words of Flaubert's mother,
Who warned him near the end of his life,
"Your mania for sentences has dried up your heart,"

And imagining the torment of Herbert Spencer,
Who spent his last days weighing the 40 years
He spent on his life's work, the 18 volumes
Of his *Synthetic Philosophy*, which he had
Piled on his lap, ". . . and as he felt their cold weight
Wondered if he would not have done better
If he had had a grandchild
In their stead."

And considering well the bloody consequences of broken words
Like Stonewall Jackson's to the Native Americans,
" . . . that our treaties will last as long
As the grass grows and rivers run free."

And recalling how Rimbaud swore off the revolt of poetry
As he died a ghoulish death in North Africa, saying plaintively,
"No more words. I can't speak anymore."

And contemplating in Istanbul's Blue Mosque the sorrow Rumi felt
After his mentor dropped all the Sufi poet's books down a well,
Followed years later by shame because he was not yet beyond language.

Still I read on until the ink speaks to me
And each word breaks down to pure sound.
I listen in for the Word
Resounding behind the word
To hear the Story
Behind the story.
I feel the screech
Of movement inside me—

Until the   tremor is felt
And the deep   white fissure
Opens on   the page
And I fall   between
The letters   in each word,
The words   in each sentence,
The sentences   in each thought,

And the Surrenders sacred chaos its meaning.

There is an ancient journey
Behind every word
That has reached us.

And so there must still be hope
For our woebegone race
If it is indeed possible
That one of us might preposterously
Cart 1000 books and 40 gallons of whiskey
Aboard a ship bound from Boston to Seattle around Cape Horn,
And pledge to read and annotate all the books
Or drink all the booze before reaching port—
And arrive at our destination
With John Barleycorn untouched,
As the story still goes in Oakland dock bars
Of their own Jack London.

Or that illiterate miners could lip-sync Pablo Neruda's poetry
During his improvised reading in a ramshackle town
High in the copper-veined mountains of Chile.

Or that Sequoyah, an untutored Cherokee, could shape
The feeling of his vision of a magical "talking leaf"
For his people into the first Indian alphabet.

Not to preserve words that burn in our memory
Is to be the servant in Saint-Simon's story
Whose job it was to follow the bishop and his mistress
Through the parish garden with a rake
And erase his master's
Footsteps.

To save them is to be the lost pilot
In the broiling desert who follows
The serpentining tracks through the mirage
Because they might lead to water
For the blackened tongue.

"For what saves a man is to take a step."

Or as Gandhi said by the spinning wheel,
"Nothing that we do matters,
But it is very important that we do it."

The first law of verbal dynamics states that
Language is in a continual state of disintegration
Where arbitrary words will fill any vacuum.

The second law of literary energy conservation states that
Nothing in language is ever truly lost, only transformed,
Imperishable if heated by the soul's blue fire.

Words are, in other words,
A means to an end,
And that end is to *mean*,

To create meaning
Where none was
Meant before.

Any *true words* you speak are poetry
That grapples with the entropy of the universe,
The inexorable breaking down of all things.

They bring you to the heart of the mystery game:
The paradox of forgetting yourself
While passing down the unforgettable.

The task of tasks is to recreate
The myth of language in a voice all your own,
Make each word yours alone.

In that boldness
Is the dreamswarm
Where the red triangle rises

Where you glide on the solar wind
To hear sweet-strange
Bird-song from your own throat

Where the seventh wave
Takes you out to sea
On a raft of coconut shells

Where the taproot is sunk so low
You hear the click of water
Rising up the bamboo shoot

Where the lion's roar
Startles you
Awake

Where the hermitage of lunatic monks
On the magic mountain gives you
Dancing lessons from God

Where the phoenix rises
So triumphantly it splinters
Your smoking mirror

Where the heartbroken fiddler
Plays the healing waltz
For your fallen brother

Where the meteor shower speaks
To you in the silver ink
Of its nightwriting

Where the tornado
Absorbs the
Shadow

Where you finally become
The clay that
Speaks

Where the tongue
The pen and the sword
Are one

And you and the nightshiftnurse with nerves
Of cool blue steel who watches you
Slowly dying, embrace.

And you can answer the troubled child who asks you,
"Why do we have souls in the bottom of our feet?"

"*So the gods can walk in our footsteps.*"

Let the darkness come.
I am learning my death chant
From the flight of cranes in the twilight sky.

I hear the green chords
Of the scarlet violin,
The perpetual emotion machine.

I follow the song
Down by the river
To the shore

Where Li Po
Was last seen trying to capture
Moonlight in his bare hands.

Chewing my next words like a warrior his arrows
To make them straight and true,
I sit on my haunches, rocking slowly,
Like a silent crow contemplating
His claw marks in the wet riverbank
And feel the evening dew on my eyes
And a slow change of tide in my blood
And see out of the corner of my eye once again: the shadow:
And hear in the ghostly lap of water at my feet

The voice of the Senegal poet,
"The dead are never gone,
They are in the shadows."

And the closing words of Monsieur Arronax
About his nemesis, Captain Nemo, in Jules Verne's
20,000 Leagues Under the Sea,
"I hoped to discover the secret of his life
In whatever last words
Might escape his lips."

And while Kane's boyhood sled burns in the castle furnace
The tantalizing image melts into the reconciling word,
"*Rosebud.*"

Apocryphal tales?
Spurious legends?
Incorrigible myth-making?

"Se non é vero, é ben trovato."
"If it's not true, it's well invented."

The rest, after all the rapturous
"Words, words, words,"
Is uncanny silence.

The shrouded night was long and full of marvels.
Now there is a murmur of dawn outside
Your window where day breaks seamlessly.
The country light wakes us with forgiveness
For some unknown sorrow, parts the dark
Doors of sleep with warm fingers,
Coaxes our eyes open in time
To catch the black wave: the morning migration
Of tens of thousands of starlings rushing
By the window in a rising current of flapping wings
And exuberant cries of joy as if they were climbing
The rising rays of the sun.

I blow out the wick in the oil lamp next to the bed.
You turn to me with eyes wet with love,

Your gaze unflinching, your desire
Taming my heart like a sorceress,
Your body sighing with sweet vulnerability.
During these naked hours together
Something is hinted at,
A strength, a perfume,
A simplicity.

Yours are soul-catcher words
Beyond books, temples, and ruins,
Words that sink moist roots in my ears,
Carry the cool consequences
Of a woman's ardent love.
What is said here is prayer.
What is not said here
Is a prism
Of emotion.

If every mystery
Longs for its image,
Mine has come home
Along this fierce trail
To feel the green force
Of love pushing through me,
Leading me on into these
Fields of rhyming light,
These skies of chiming color,
To find the ancient honey
Of your sweet
Swirling tongue.

It is astonishing
how we found
each other.

Now I can remember to forget my forgetting.
The first palimpsest has peeled back.
The last mask has vanished.
The gold coins have been tossed.

The sphinx has been answered.
The light pours from my pen.

This is the decisive moment
When I know I can improvise
My own last words.

And in that ever-echoing moment,
I can hear his last goodbye to me,
I can imagine the promise
Of my father's last words
In a telephone call
With my uncle,

"*Can we carry on this conversation*
some other
time—"

Thoughts count
Stories matter
Words last

What could not be said then
Drives me on now
Despite myself

As I carry on
The long
Conversation

And word by word
Awake and stretch
For the longest stride

And my own shadow
Lengthens
On the bronze sundial

And raises the stone
Tower stone by rising
Stone

And I carefully
Place the tale back
Where I found it

And riverwater
In underground caves
Dissolves stone
And shapes
Subterranean
Cathedrals

Of blazing
Heart red
Minerals

PHIL COUSINEAU
Berkeley-Paris-San Francisco
1983–1990

NOTES ON DEADLINES

Since I was a boy I have been a quotemonger. Inspired by my father's passion for his library and wordgames, I have gathered thousands of memorable lines from baseball to science fiction, mythology to literature, ones that *hummed* to me like telegraph lines. Over the years he sent me hundreds of books, magazines, and articles, many with index cards inserted into them with aphorisms, jokes, or famous last words scrawled, until his last illness, in his firm, sergeant-straight red marker printing.

But it wasn't until the early 1980s when I began to teach that I began to organize my favorite quotes into a collection that I called "Montaigne's Quotehangar," in whimsical deference to the French essayist's famous epigram, "I quote others only to express myself better."

That collection was divided into categories like Art, Poetry, Love, Literature, Mythology, Art, Film, Sports, War, and many others, including Collective Nouns, Limericks, and Last Words. No sooner did the pattern emerge then, serendipitously enough, a multitude of famous—and infamous—last words began coming my way, as if they were now collecting me.

From biographies, newspaper stories, encyclopedias, and anecdotes culled from friends in cafés, the collection grew. Eventually I found compilations like Barnaby Conrad's *Famous Last Words*, *Proust's Last Beer* by Bob Arnebeck and Allen Appel, *Brewer's Dictionary of Phrase and Fable*, Jonathon Green's *Famous Last Words*, and *The Last Word* by Gyles Brandreth. I was also inspired and delighted by the Milwaukee poet Antler's amazing "Last Words," the title poem from his visionary first collection of bardic poetry.

I am indebted to these works and the other countless sources I used to verify the dying sayings and literary anecdotes included here, all those that ignited in me the critical movement from compilation to contemplation of the soulful relationship between death and language, love and death.

I

Page

4. *The strong time* is a term used by mythologist Mircea Eliade in reference to the primordial moments or eras when we're no longer in chronological time, "the prodigious, 'sacred' time when something *new*, *strong*, and *significant* was manifested."
6. *The Eleusinian Mysteries* were an annual religious ritual of rebirth dating back to the Bronze Age at the shrine of Eleusis, near Athens.
8. *St. John of the Cross* was a 16th-century Carmelite friar imprisoned in a monastery dungeon in Toledo, Spain, where he wrote mystical poems including *Dark Night of the Soul. Miguel Cervantes* (1547–1616) was said to have written *Don Quixote*, a quest romance often regarded as the first novel, while in prison. *Andrei Sakharov* was a physicist, author, and Nobel Peace Prize winner in 1975 from the Soviet Union. *Viktor Frankl* was imprisoned at Auschwitz during World War II and later wrote an indelibly moving account of his incarceration, *Man's Search for Meaning*.
10. The *rancher* referred to is Charles Goodnight and the story is recounted in his *Indian Recollections*.
12. The *gulag prisoner* is Raoul Wallenberg. He was sentenced to life in a Siberian prison camp after the armistice in the second world war after saving an estimated 30,000 Jews from Hitler's purge in Germany.
13. The French author, *Claude Simon*, won the Nobel Prize for Literature in 1985 for his experimental war novel, *The Flanders Road*, which explores several perspectives of one soldier's death.
14. The poet of these lines is Hugo Von Hofmanstaal (1874–1929). The line *When I have fears . . .* is from John Keats (1795–1821), but I first came across them in Adrienne Rich's marvelous poem, "To a Poet," where she paraphrased him: *"and you have fears that you will cease to be before your pen has glean'd your teeming brain"*. I have written both versions of these eminently inspiring lines on many a blackboard for my writing students.

II

25. Another version of the last words of the poet *John Keats* is: "Severn, lift me up, I'm dying. I shall die easy; don't be frightened—be firm, and thank God it has come." Yet another version of is actually Keats' epitaph: "Here lies one whose name is writ on water."
26. A second choice for the last utterings of *Rabelais*, the French satirist (c. 1490–1553): "Ring down the curtain, the farce is over," a variation on the last ones of the Roman emperor Augustus is, "Do you think I have played my part pretty well through the farce of life?" Another report of the last words of *Thomas Hobbes* (1588–1679), the

English philosopher: "I shall be glad then to find a hole to creep out of the world at."

28. *The mesmerizing cry* . . . is from Mevlana Jalal-uddin Rumi (1207–73), the mystic poet and founder of the dervish movement from Persia.

III

37. The *sensei* quoted was the martial arts teacher of Japanese baseball superstar Sadharu Oh, as honored in his book *Sadharu Oh*, a splendid blend of spiritual and athletic autobiography.
38. *The old translater* is Father Francisco Ximinez of the Santo Tomas Chuila parish of Mexico who discovered the long-lost manuscript of the *Popol Vuh* in 1737. He copied the *Quiche Maya* and made the first translation into Spanish, saying that the myth was "the doctrine which they first imbibed with their mother's milk," and that all of them knew it by heart. His version lay unpublished for 150 years until discovered at the University of San Carlos in Guatemala, then finally published in Vienna in 1857.
    The golden bough is a reference to Aeneas in Greek mythology. In Virgil's *Aeneid* our hero is lost when his pilot Palinaurus is drowned. The Sibyl tells him she will lead him to his dead father in the underworld if he will find the golden bough, without which there can be no entrance into the land of Hades. The implication is as intriguing today as it was then: we need an amulet for our descent into the depths.
39. "*Tell me, mother, the word known to all men*" and "*Love, the word known to all men*" (page 100, line 24) are long-missing lines from James Joyce's *Ulysses*, two of roughly 6000 printer's mistakes finally corrected in the reconstructed edition of 1986.

V

51. "*Australian aborigine shamans say* . . . " These are lines from a traditional Australian aborigine song.
56. "*Life must be understood* . . . " is an epigram by Ludwig Wittgenstein (1889–1951), the Austrian philosopher.
60. *The harrower of hell*'s oft-quoted lines are from Corinthians (I:55).
    The little girl in the Looking Glass is, of course, Louis Carroll's "dreamchild," Alice.
    What is it? . . . " This triptych is based on a curious coincidence one day in 1983 when I read Alan Watts' *This is It* in the morning and played basketball with a group of dazzling black players in the afternoon, one of whom kept shouting, "What it *is*!" after every flamboyant basket.

61. A *coelacanth* is a peculiar five-and-a-half foot long prehistoric fish, thought to have been extinct since the Cretaceous period, yet rediscovered in 1938 off the coast of Africa by a fisherman. Several others have been found since.
Oubliettes: from the French *oublier*: to forget, literally then, a prisoner's cell for those to be forgotten forever.

VI

75. The *minotaur* is Spanish painter Pablo Picasso (1881–1973), evoked most memorably in the images from the "Vuillard Suites."

VII

79. A variation of the second century B.C. philosopher Archimedes' last words is "Wait till I have finished my problem."
80. An alternate to the last thoughts of the French encyclopediast Diderot (1713–1784): "The first step towards philosophy is incredulity."
83. *The haunted ink bottle* is a reference to the 19th century Irish dramatist and wit Oscar Wilde.
84. *The muse-intoxicated dramatist* is the classical writer Euripides (c480–406?BC).

VIII

85. "*I have no time to die; I have too many deadlines*" is a lifeline offered to us from Nicolas Slonimsky and his book *Lexicon of Musical Invective: Critical Assaults on Composers since Beethoven*. Compare the entertainer George Burns: "I can't afford to die; I'm all booked up."
90. A second version of *Oscar Wilde*'s last words is, "Either the wallpaper goes, or I do."
91. *The sly fool* is again filmmaker Woody Allen.
93. A *powder monkey* is an explosives expert.
97. *Ram*, Ghandi's conscious invocation of one of the many Hindu names for God at the moment of his assassination, is a reflection of the Hindu belief that dying with God's name on your lips enables you to return to the source of all creation. *Ram* is also a Sanskrit mantra associated with the seat of power in the solar plexus, and the name of the gateway to the heart shakra, the seat of the individual's sound.
98. The story of *Alfred Kroeber* is recounted in Theodora Kroeber's engaging biography of her husband, *Configurations*.
100. The *nine-domed cathedral* referred to is Saint-Front in Perigueux, France, the home of my ancestor, Jean-Baptiste Cousineau. Family

tradition has it that he left for Canada and the New World in 1678. I like to imagine his prayers still echoing in the domes. *N'oubliez pas l'amour* is translated into English as: "Do not forget about love."

IX

105. The doctrine of signatures first appears in the work of German mystic Jacob Boehme (1574–1624) and later in the long poem "The Signature of All Things," by American poet Kenneth Rexroth.
106. The story of *Herbert Spencer* (1820–1903) is recounted by the modern Chinese historian Lin Yutang.
107. *The lost pilot* refers to French author and war hero Antoine St. Exupery. His adventures are brilliantly recounted in such books as *Wind, Sand and the Stars.*
110. *Li Po* (701–762) was a Chinese poet-philosopher during the Tang dynasty.
111. "*Words, words, words . . .* ", after "Hamlet," by William Shakespeare.

ABOUT THE AUTHOR

Phil Cousineau was born at Fort Jackson, Columbia, South Carolina, in 1952, and grew up in Wayne, Michigan. While working nightshift in an automotive parts factory he studied at the University of Detroit, graduating in 1974 with a degree in journalism. Since then he has traveled widely around the world, living in England, Ireland, France, Israel, and the Philippines, and worked variously as a freelance writer, housepainter, art and literary tour leader, kibbutz farmhand, teacher and lecturer, and documentary film scriptwriter.

He is cowriter and associate producer of the award-winning film, *The Hero's Journey: the World of Joseph Campbell*, author of its companion book, *The Hero's Journey: The Life and Work of Joseph Campbell* (Harper & Row), and worked with John Densmore on his autobiography, *Riders on the Storm: My Life with Jim Morrison and The Doors* (Delacorte Press).

Currently he lives in San Francisco, California.

ABOUT THE ARTIST

Robin Eschner can be found most often in Sonoma County, California where she lives with her daughter Heather, their three-legged dog Bear, and his many furry four-legged peers. Work time there is divided between painting and printmaking in the studio which has come to be known by accepting friends as Sky Turtle Lodge.

Since graduating from the University of California at Davis in 1976, Robin's work has been shown extensively throughout the United States in various exhibitions and reproduced internationally in books and calendars and as fine art cards and posters.

ACKNOWLEDGEMENTS

My heartfelt thanks to all those who helped me finally bring this book home, especially Eric Johnson of Okeanos Press in Oakland, California for his masterly design, guidance, and patience, and Robin Eschner for the mysterious gift of her haunting woodcuts that edged a book about words beyonds words.

To those friends and family who read—and reread—the innumerable drafts of the manuscript over the years and offered their suggestions and encouragement, notably my brother Paul Cousineau, Trish O'Rielly, Lynne Kaufman, Yasha Aginsky, Jeff Poniewaz, and Antler, I want to convey my deepest gratitude. And to George Whitman of Shakespeare and Company Bookstore in Paris, thanks for the two-month sabbatical in the Writer's Room of your Rag and Bone Shop of the Heart. Many thanks also to Jo Beaton for her help in putting the shoulder to the boulder while setting up Sisyphus Press.

Finally, it feels apropro to acknowledge the other unacknowledged legislators of the world, the café owners who offered me the traditional writer's second home when cabin fever set in, especially those who poured the cappuccinos, cafe lattes, and chiantis for me at Cafe Roma in Berkeley, La Coupole in Paris, and Mario's Bohemian Cigar Store in North Beach, San Francisco.

Critical Praise for Phil Cousineau's DEADLINES

"Illuminating, witty, sometimes shocking—more than a catalog of last words—this is a meditation on death, beautifully expressed for every lover of Words."

NOEL RILEY FITCH, author of
Sylvia Beach and the Lost Generation
and *Walks in Hemingway's Paris*

"A marvelously experimental effervescence of poetry and prose dedicated to the wisdom, despair, joy, irreverence, and deep longings expressed over the centuries by men and women facing themselves at the moment of death. *Deadlines* confronts the quintessential question facing us all in the '90s as we witness the going of our own untenable way of life on earth. Cousineau has the remarkable ability to uncover the gift of the new even as the old life recedes."

DAVID WHYTE, English poet, author of
Songs of Coming Home, and *Where Two Rivers Meet*

"*Deadlines* is a remarkable epic prose poem shaped around the dying words of the famous and infamous. . . . Try *not* to be moved by the sheer soulful weight of Cousineau's extended meditation on words spoken at the moment of *crossing over*. . . ."

KEITH THOMPSON, *Utne Reader*

"Phil Cousineau writes as a Seer who gazes at the very juncture between life and death, which our culture profoundly ignores. His poetic meditation on 'Famous Last Words' serves as a finely crafted mirror reflecting encoded glimpses of illumination—what is remembered and what is inevitably lost in our unavoidable transition into death. This is an exquisite celebration of life and its cherished epiphanies, beautifully illustrated by Robin Eschner's woodcuts."

JOAN MARLER, KPFA poetry editor and programmer

"Cousineau is a consummate and passionate wordman, and the subject of the appointment with the Big D.—Death—and his thoughts about last words are totally compelling. I've lost a lot of people in my life and this blood-n-guts epic prose poem gives me some consolation about 'The End.'"

JOHN DENSMORE, the drummer for The Doors,
author of *Riders on the Storm:*
My Life with Jim Morrison and The Doors

"I loved *Deadlines*. It's very passionate, erudite, funny, wise and a delicious distillation of language. The weaving of famous last words with Cousineau's own insights and experiences is masterful. It's a very rich, dense book that will bear many re-readings. I was particularly moved by the injunction to live your life fully: 'What are you waiting for?' I would suggest that people buy the book *now*: 'What are you waiting for?'"

LYNNE KAUFMAN, playwright, *The Couch, Speaking in Tongues, Our Lady of the Desert*

"Cousineau writes with authority, grace and power. It's a pleasure to read him in a context where he can let it rip and rock and roll. All night long. *Deadlines* is a provocative and enlightening book."

DANNY SUGERMAN, coauthor of *No One Here Gets Out Alive*, and author of *Wonderland Avenue*

"A large tapestry of human ideas transformed to a suspension bridge over once abandoned roads. *Deadlines* guides us along the paths of others toward the trailhead of what we call death, revealing us to ourselves as naked in the procession of destiny. It merges mortal visions into an epic panorama of life."

ANGELA BROWNE MILLER, psychotherapist, lecturer at University of California at Berkeley, author of *Working Dazed*

"Phil Cousineau's creativity is taking many forms. This is a root source that readers will enjoy."

STANLEY KELEMAN, author of *Living Your Dying*

"*Deadlines* is a compression of many journeys into one. It is a Dantesque walk with death, a psalm for the ages, a Joycean 'Here comes everybody.' We feel ourselves in the presence of an ancient bard who holds the key to our forgotten past. This long poem, beautifully illustrated by Robin Eschner, reminds me of Castiglioni's *Book of the Courier* where men and women speak of love and death all night; the sun rises and the company parts, shyly, gratefully, having shared the deepest secrets of their souls. Cousineau has accomplished the highest form of storytelling: he has shown us what lies between beauty and terror. The gods have truly given him the gift."

VALERIE ANDREWS, author of *A Passion for This Earth*